101 Double-Ended Hook Stitches

With techniques as lovely and simple as Crochet On the Double™ and Crochenit® it is a foregone conclusion that a reference book of stitch patterns should be produced. Included are closely woven stitch patterns to the more open and lacy Crochenit stitches. A photograph of each side of the swatch demonstrates which stitches work best for reversible designs. All you need to determine is whether to make a dishcloth, place mat, afghan or a wearable garment.

CROCHENIT HOOK

Double-ended hooks come in a variety of sizes, most commonly D through P, and are available as a double-ended straight hook and with a cable

General Information

Many of the products used in this pattern book can be purchased from local craft, fabric and variety stores or from the Annie's Attic catalog.

These 101 stitch patterns are ideal for creating anything from sweaters to tissue covers, place mats to afghans. All sizes and weights of yarn can be used with this technique.

Once you choose a project and a stitch pattern, the next step is to determine the gauge and hook size to use.

DOUBLE-ENDED SIZE G HOOK

Crochet on the Double Swivel hooks are available at AnniesAttic.com and ease in stitching large projects. If you are making an afghan, determine if you want the stitches to have a closer weave like a fabric, or a more open weave to the design.

Shown here, on pages 2 and 3, you can see three gauge samples, all using same pattern, and three diverse hook sizes. The same stitch pattern takes on a different texture and look in proportion to the size of the hook used.

crochenit tips

Use the red and green stoppers to help you keep track of when you turn your hook and which end of the hook you work with on any row. As you turn your hook each time, remove the stopper and place it on the opposite end of the hook.

Before you lay your work aside, work until you have loops on hook.

Turn hook, place the green stopper on the end of the hook with which you will begin next tIme, and place the red stopper on the other end. Red means "Stop" and green means "Go!"

When you pick your work up again, you can start right away without having to figure out which end is the beginning. The stoppers also keep your work from sliding off your hook.

Insert hook in 2nd chain from hook, yarn over and through *(see photo A)*, leaving loop on hook,

Holding the double-end hook like a knife makes it easier to use.

*to **draw up a loop**, insert hook in next chain, yarn over and draw through; repeat from * across *(see photo B)*, leaving all loops on hook,

drop color A, turn hook and slide all loops to opposite end of hook *(see photo C)*.

*Each of these loops counts as a stitch and is referred to as a **vertical bar**.*

To **work loops off hook,** with color B, place slip knot on hook *(see photo D)*,

draw slip knot through first loop on hook *(see photo E)*,

Pulling the slip knot through the first loop makes the first stitch of the row.

yarn over, draw through next 2 loops on hook *(see photo F)*,

*When you pull through the 2 loops in this step, you will go through 1 loop of each color. The stitches you are making in this step are referred to as **horizontal bar**.*

to **work remaining loops off hook,** (yarn over, draw through next 2 loops on hook) across, leaving last loop on hook *(see photo G)*, **do not turn**.

You will now have only 1 loop on your hook. This loop counts as the first vertical bar of the next row. Never turn after working the loops off your hook.

FIRST VERTICAL BAR

Skip first vertical bar, insert hook under next vertical bar, yarn over and draw up a loop *(see photo H)*,

draw up a loop in each vertical bar across, drop color B *(see photo I)*,

If you have trouble with your loops falling off the hook, cap the unused end with a rubber knit stopper or a piece of cork.

turn and slide all loops to opposite end of hook *(see photo J)*.

To keep your yarn from tangling when you turn, rotate your hook back and forth rather than in a circle.

Pick up color A from row below, yarn over and draw through first loop on hook *(see photo K)*,

This is the same process as in step E, except you are using the yarn from the row below rather than placing a slip knot on the hook.

yarn over, draw through next 2 loops on hook *(see photo L)*;

Remember to go through 1 loop of each color when working the loops off in this step.

to **work remaining loops off hook,** (yarn over and draw through next 2 loops on hook) across, leaving last loop on hook, **do not turn** (see photo M).

Skip first vertical bar, draw up loop in next vertical bar (see photo N), draw up loop in each bar across, drop color A, turn. Slide all loops to opposite end of hook.

Continue alternating colors until ending with color A (or color specified in individual pattern instructions).

Skip first vertical bar, slip stitch (or use the stitch called for in the individual pattern instructions) across (see photo O). Fasten off.

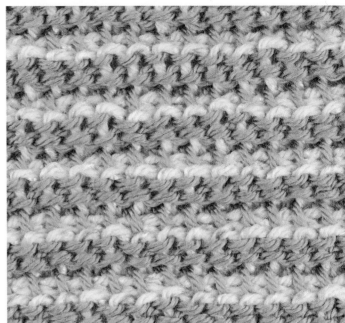

MATERIALS
- Medium (worsted) weight yarn:
  1 oz/50 yds/28g 2 colors A and B
- H/8/5mm double-ended hook used for
  photographed block

4 MEDIUM

PATTERN NOTE
Read General Instructions on pages 5–7 before
beginning pattern.

INSTRUCTIONS
STITCH PATTERN
Row 1: With color A, ch 21 or desired number of sts,
pull up lp in 2nd ch from hook, pull up lp in each ch
across, turn. *(21 lps on hook)*

Row 2: With color B, work lps off hook, **do not turn**.

Row 3: Sk first vertical bar, pull up lp in each vertical
bar across, turn.

Row 4: With color A, work lps off hook, **do not turn**.

Row 5: Rep row 3.

Rows 6–34: [Rep rows 2–5 consecutively] 8 times,
ending last rep with row 2.

Row 35: Ch 1, sk first vertical bar, sl st in each vertical
bar across. Fasten off. ■

design by Mary Middleton

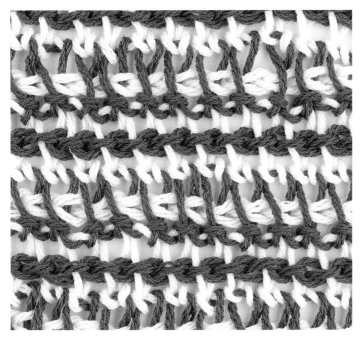

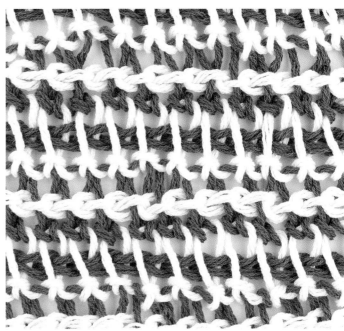

MATERIALS
- Medium (worsted) weight yarn:
  1 oz/50 yds/28g 2 colors A and B
- Crochenit hook used for
  photographed block

4 **MEDIUM**

PATTERN NOTE
Read General Instructions on pages 5–7 before beginning pattern.

SPECIAL STITCH
High stitch (high st): Insert hook in next vertical bar or in place indicated, yo, pull lp through, ch 1.

INSTRUCTIONS
STITCH PATTERN
Row 1: With color A, ch 18 or desired number of sts, pull up lp in 3rd ch from hook, ch 1 *(high st completed)*, **high st** *(see Special Stitch)* in each ch across, turn. *(17 high sts)*

Row 2: With color B, work lps off hook, **do not turn**.

Row 3: Ch 1, sk first vertical bar, high st in each vertical bar across, turn.

Row 4: With color A, work lps off hook, **do not turn**.

Row 5: Ch 1, sk first vertical bar, high st in each vertical bar across, turn.

Rows 6–16: [Rep rows 2–5 consecutively] 3 times, ending last rep with row 4.

Row 17: Ch 1, sk first vertical bar, sl st in each vertical bar across. Fasten off. ∎

number 3

design by Carolyn Christmas

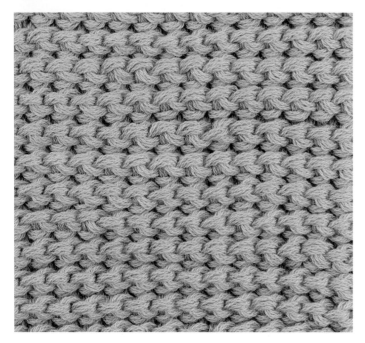

MATERIALS

- Medium (worsted) weight yarn:
  1 oz/50 yds/28g 2 colors A and B
- H/8/5mm double-ended hook used for photographed block

4 MEDIUM

PATTERN NOTE

Read General Instructions on pages 5–7 before beginning pattern.

INSTRUCTIONS

STITCH PATTERN

Row 1: With color A, ch 18 or desired number of sts, pull up lp in 2nd ch from hook, pull up lp in each ch across, turn. *(18 lps on hook)*

Row 2: With color B, work lps off hook, **do not turn.**

Row 3: Ch 1, sk first vertical bar, pull up lp in sp under next **horizontal bar** *(see illustration)*, pull up lp in sp under each horizontal bar across, turn.

Horizontal Bar

Row 4: With color A, work lps off hook, **do not turn.**

Row 5: Rep row 3.

Rows 6–56: [Rep rows 2–5 consecutively] 13 times, ending last rep with row 4.

Row 57: Ch 1, sk first vertical bar, sl st in sl st in sp under each horizontal bar across. Fasten off. ■

number 4

design by Ann Parnell

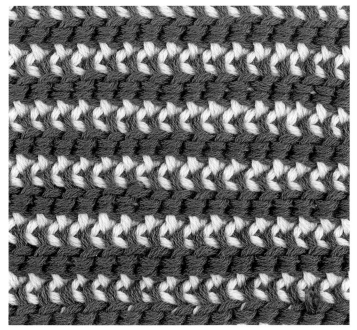

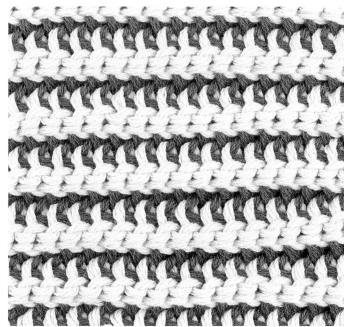

MATERIALS
- Medium (worsted) weight yarn:
  1 oz/50 yds/28g 2 colors A and B
- H/8/5mm double-ended hook used for photographed block

4 MEDIUM

PATTERN NOTE
Read General Instructions on pages 5–7 before beginning pattern.

INSTRUCTIONS
STITCH PATTERN
Row 1: With color A, ch 21 or desired number of sts, pull up lp in 2nd ch from hook, pull up lp in each ch across, turn. *(21 lps on hook)*

Row 2: With color B, work lps off hook, **do not turn**.

Row 3: Ch 1, pull up lp in top strand of first **horizontal bar** *(see illustration)*, pull up lp in top strand of each horizontal bar across, turn.

Horizontal Bar

Row 4: With color A, work lps off hook, **do not turn**.

Row 5: Rep row 3.

Rows 6–28: [Rep rows 2–5 consecutively] 6 times, ending last rep with row 4.

Row 29: Ch 1, sk first vertical bar, sl st in top strand of each horizontal bar across. Fasten off. ■

design by Ann Parnell

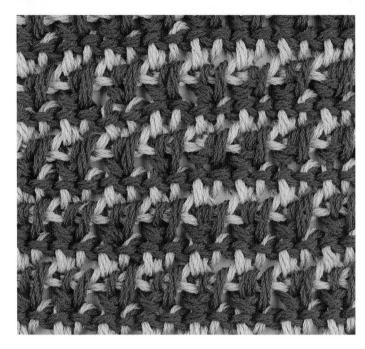

MATERIALS

- Medium (worsted) weight yarn:
  1 oz/50 yds/28g 2 colors A and B
- H/8/5mm double-ended hook used for
  photographed block

4 MEDIUM

PATTERN NOTE

Read General Instructions on pages 5–7 before
beginning pattern.

INSTRUCTIONS

STITCH PATTERN

Row 1: With color A, ch 22 or even number of sts,
pull up lp in 2nd ch from hook, pull up lp in each ch
across, turn. *(22 lps on hook)*

Row 2: With color B, work lps off hook, **do not turn**.

Row 3: Ch 1, pull up lp in top strand
of first **horizontal bar** *(see illustration)*,
[yo, sk next horizontal bar, pull up lp
in top strand of next horizontal bar]
across, turn.

Horizontal Bar

Row 4: With color A, work lps off hook, **do not turn**.

Row 5: Rep row 3.

Rows 6–28: [Rep rows 2–5 consecutively] 6 times,
ending last rep with row 4.

Row 29: Ch 1, sk first vertical bar, sl st in top strand
of each horizontal bar across. Fasten off. ■

number 6

design by Ann Parnell

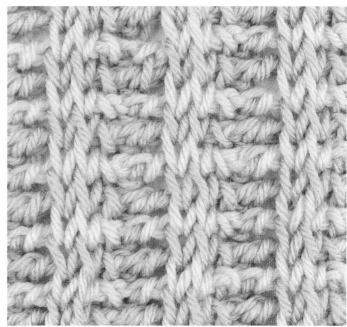

MATERIALS
- Medium (worsted) weight yarn:
  1 oz/50 yds/28g 2 colors A and B
- H/8/5mm double-ended hook used for photographed block

4 MEDIUM

PATTERN NOTE
Read General Instructions on pages 5–7 before beginning pattern.

SPECIAL STITCHES
Knit: Insert hook between front and back vertical bars and under horizontal bar of next st *(see illustration)*, yo, pull up lp.

Knit Stitch

Purl: Holding yarn in front of work and hook at back of work, insert hook from back to front through back and front vertical bars of next st, yo, pull up lp.

INSTRUCTIONS
STITCH PATTERN
Row 1: With color A, ch 22 or in multiples of 4 plus 2 chs, pull up lp in 2nd ch from hook, pull up lp in each ch across, turn. *(22 lps on hook)*

Row 2: With color B, work lps off hook, **do not turn**.

Row 3: Sk first vertical bar, **knit** *(see Special Stitches)* 1, **purl** *(see Special Stitches)* 2, knit 2, [purl 2, knit 2] across, turn.

Row 4: With color A, work lps off hook, **do not turn**.

Row 5: Sk first vertical bar, purl 1, [knit 2, purl 2] across, turn.

Rows 6–36: [Rep rows 2–5 consecutively] 8 times, ending last rep with row 4.

Row 37: Ch 1, sk first vertical bar, sl st in each vertical bar across. Fasten off. ■

design by Ann Parnell

MATERIALS
- Medium (worsted) weight yarn:
  1 oz/50 yds/28g 2 colors A and B
- H/8/5mm double-ended hook used for photographed block

4 MEDIUM

PATTERN NOTE
Read General Instructions on pages 5–7 before beginning pattern.

SPECIAL STITCHES
Knit: Insert hook between front and back vertical bars and under horizontal bar of next st *(see illustration)*, yo, pull up lp.

Knit Stitch

Purl: Holding yarn in front of work and hook at back of work, insert hook from back to front through back and front vertical bars of next st, yo, pull up lp.

INSTRUCTIONS

STITCH PATTERN
Row 1: With color A, ch 20 or in multiples of 6 plus 2 chs, pull up lp in 2nd ch from hook, pull up lp in each ch across, turn. *(20 lps on hook)*

Row 2: With color B, work lps off hook, **do not turn**.

Row 3: Sk first vertical bar, **knit** *(see Special Stitches)* 2, **purl** *(see Special Stitches)* 2, [knit 4, purl 2] twice, knit 3, turn.

Row 4: With color A, work lps off hook, **do not turn**.

Row 5: Sk first vertical bar, purl 2, knit 2, [purl 4, knit 2] twice, purl 3, turn.

Rows 6–34: [Rep rows 2–5 consecutively] 8 times, ending last rep with row 2.

Row 35: Ch 1, sk first vertical bar, sl st in each vertical bar across. Fasten off. ■

number 8

design by Ann Parnell

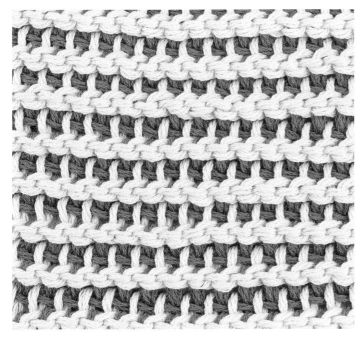

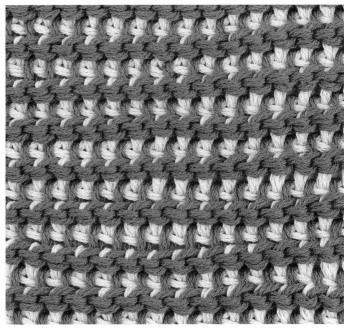

MATERIALS

- Medium (worsted) weight yarn:
  1 oz/50 yds/28g 2 colors A and B
- H/8/5mm double-ended hook used for photographed block

4 MEDIUM

PATTERN NOTE

Read General Instructions on pages 5–7 before beginning pattern.

INSTRUCTIONS

STITCH PATTERN

Row 1: With color A, ch 21 or desired number of sts, pull up lp in 2nd ch from hook, pull up lp in each ch across, turn. *(21 lps on hook)*

Row 2: With color B, work lps off hook, **do not turn**.

Row 3: Ch 1, sk first vertical bar, pull up lp under top 2 strands of next **horizontal bar** *(see illustration)*, pull up lp under top 2 strands of each horizontal bar across, turn.

Horizontal Bar

Row 4: With color A, work lps off hook, **do not turn**.

Row 5: Rep row 3.

Rows 6–38: [Rep rows 2–5 consecutively] 9 times, ending last rep with row 2.

Row 39: Ch 1, sk first vertical bar, sl st under top 2 strands of each horizontal bar across. Fasten off. ■

design by Dorris Brooks

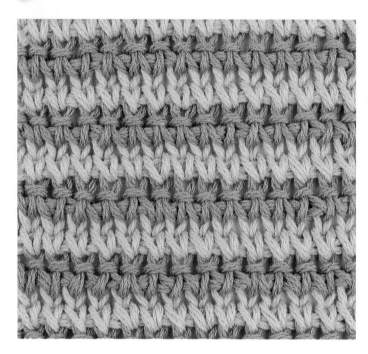

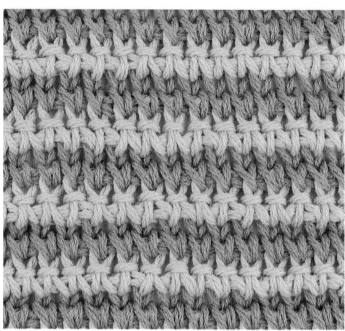

MATERIALS
- Medium (worsted) weight yarn:
  1 oz/50 yds/28g 2 colors A and B
- H/8/5mm double-ended hook used for photographed block

4 MEDIUM

PATTERN NOTE
Read General Instructions on pages 5–7 before beginning pattern.

SPECIAL STITCH
Knit: Insert hook between front and back vertical bars and under horizontal bar of next st *(see illustration)*, yo, pull up lp.

Knit Stitch

INSTRUCTIONS

STITCH PATTERN
Row 1: With color A, ch 19 or desired number of sts, pull up lp in 2nd ch from hook, ch 1, [pull up lp in next ch, ch 1] across, turn. *(19 lps on hook)*

Row 2: With color B, work lps off hook, **do not turn**.

Row 3: Ch 1, sk first vertical bar, **knit** *(see Special Stitch)* 1, ch 1, [knit 1, ch 1] across, turn.

Row 4: With color A, work lps off hook, *do not turn*.

Row 5: Rep row 3.

Rows 6–38: [Rep rows 2–5 consecutively] 9 times, ending last rep with row 2.

Row 39: Working in vertical bars same as for knit, ch 1, sk first vertical bar, sc in each vertical bar across. Fasten off. ■

design by Jennifer McClain

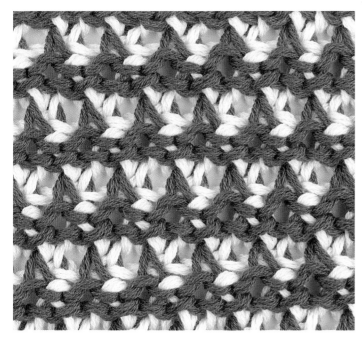

MATERIALS

- Medium (worsted) weight yarn:
  1 oz/50 yds/28g 2 colors A and B
- Size H/8/5mm double-ended hook used
  for photographed block

4 MEDIUM

PATTERN NOTE

Read General Instructions on pages 5–7 before
beginning pattern.

INSTRUCTIONS

STITCH PATTERN

Row 1: With color A, ch 20 or even number of chs,
pull up lp in 2nd ch from hook, pull up lp in each ch
across, turn. *(20 lps on hook)*

Row 2: With color B, work lps off hook, **do not turn**.

Row 3: Ch 1, *pull up lp in top strand
of next **horizontal bar** *(see illustration)*,
insert hook under next 2 vertical bars
at same time, yo, pull up lp, rep from *
across to last horizontal bar, pull up lp in
top strand of last horizontal bar, turn.

Horizontal Bar

Row 4: With color A, work lps off hook, **do not turn**.

Row 5: Rep row 3.

Row 6: With color B, work lps off hook.

Row 7: Ch 1, pull up lp in top strand of each of first 2
horizontal bars, [insert hook under next 2 vertical bars
at same time, yo, pull up lp, pull up lp in top strand of
next horizontal bar] across to last 2 vertical bars, pull
up lp in top strand of last horizontal bar, turn.

Row 8: With color A, work lps off hook, **do not turn**.

Row 9: Rep row 7.

Rows 10–22: [Rep rows 2–9 consecutively] twice,
ending last rep with row 6 and color B.

Row 23: Ch 1, sl st in top strand of each of next 2
horizontal bars, [sl st in next 2 vertical bars at same
time, sl st in top strand of next horizontal bar] across.
Fasten off. ■

design by Joyce Nordstrom

MATERIALS
- Medium (worsted) weight yarn:
  1 oz/50 yds/28g 3 colors (A, B, & C)
- Size H/8/5mm double-ended hook used
  for photographed block

4 MEDIUM

PATTERN NOTE
Read General Instructions on pages 5–7 before beginning pattern.

SPECIAL STITCH
Double crochet loop (dc lp): Yo, pull up lp in next vertical bar, yo, pull through 2 lps on hook.

INSTRUCTIONS
STITCH PATTERN
Row 1: With A, ch 40 or in multiples of 19 plus 21, pull up lp in 2nd ch from hook and in each ch across, turn. *(40 lps on hook)*

Row 2: With B, work lps off hook, **do not turn**.

Row 3: Sk first 2 vertical bars, **dc lp** *(see Special Stitch)* in each of next 8 vertical bars, dc lp in top strand of

next **horizontal bar** *(see illustration)*, dc lp in next vertical bar, dc lp in next horizontal bar, dc lp in each of next 8 vertical bars, [sk next 2 vertical bars, dc lp in each of next 8 vertical bars, dc lp in top strand of next horizontal bar, dc lp in next vertical bar, dc lp in next horizontal bar, dc lp in each of next 8 vertical bars] across to last 2 vertical bars, sk next vertical bar, dc lp in last vertical bar, turn.

Horizontal Bar

Row 4: With A, work lps off hook, **do not turn**.

Row 5: Rep row 3.

Row 6: With C, work lps off hook, **do not turn**.

Row 7: Rep row 3.

Row 8: With A, work lps off hook, **do not turn**.

Row 9: Rep row 3.

Next rows: Rep rows 2–9 consecutively, ending with row 8. At end of last row, fasten off. ■

number 12

design by Mary Middleton

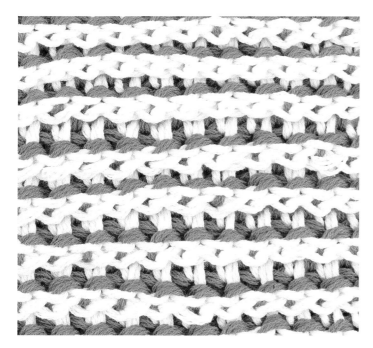
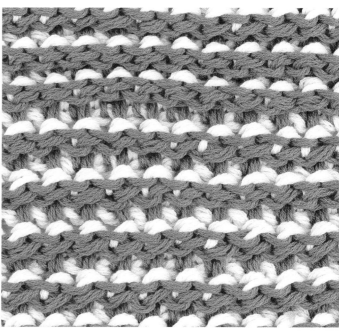

MATERIALS
- Medium (worsted) weight yarn:
  1 oz/50 yds/28g 2 colors A and B
- Crochenit hook used for
  photographed block

PATTERN NOTE
Read General Instructions on pages 5–7 before beginning pattern.

INSTRUCTIONS
STITCH PATTERN
Row 1: With color A, ch 18 or desired number of chs, pull up lp in 2nd ch from hook, pull up lp in each ch across, turn. *(18 lps on hook)*

Row 2: With color B, work lps off hook, **do not turn**.

Row 3: Ch 1, sk first vertical bar, pull up lp around both lps of next vertical bar, pull up lp around both lps of each vertical bar across, turn.

Row 4: With color A, work lps off hook, **do not turn**.

Row 5: Rep row 3.

Rows 6–56: [Rep rows 2–5 consecutively] 13 times, ending last rep with row 4.

Row 57: Ch 1, sk first vertical bar, sl st around both lps of each vertical bar across. Fasten off. ■

design by Mary Middleton

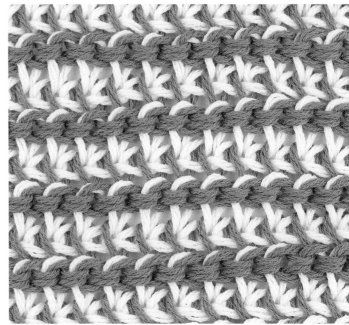

MATERIALS
- Medium (worsted) weight yarn:
  1 oz/50 yds/28g 2 colors A and B
- Crochenit hook used for
  photographed block

4 MEDIUM

PATTERN NOTE
Read General Instructions on pages 5–7 before
beginning pattern.

SPECIAL STITCH
Rib stitch (rib st): Insert hook in next
vertical bar and under top strand of
next **horizontal bar** *(see illustration)* at
same time, yo, pull lp through.

Horizontal Bar

INSTRUCTIONS
STITCH PATTERN
Row 1: With color A, ch 19 or desired number of chs,
pull up lp in 2nd ch from hook, pull up lp in each ch
across, turn. *(19 lps on hook)*

Row 2: With color B, work lps off hook, **do not turn.**

Row 3: Ch 1, sk first vertical bar, **rib st** *(see Special
Stitch)* in each st across to last vertical bar, pull up lp
in last vertical bar, turn.

Row 4: With color A, work lps off hook, **do not turn.**

Row 5: Rep row 3.

Rows 6–40: [Rep rows 2–5 consecutively] 9 times,
ending last rep with row 4.

Row 41: Ch 1, sk first vertical bar, [sl st in next
vertical bar and under top strand of next horizontal
bar at same time] across to last vertical bar, sl st in
last vertical bar. Fasten off. ■

design by Mary Middleton

MATERIALS

- Medium (worsted) weight yarn:
  1 oz/50 yds/28g 2 colors A and B
- Crochenit hook used for
  photographed block

4 MEDIUM

PATTERN NOTE

Read General Instructions on pages 5–7 before beginning pattern.

SPECIAL STITCH

Slip through stitch (sl through st): Insert hook through next 2 verticals bars at same time, yo, pull through 1 bar.

INSTRUCTIONS

STITCH PATTERN

Row 1: With color A, ch 19 or odd number of chs, pull up lp in 2nd ch from hook, pull up lp in each ch across, turn. *(19 lps on hook)*

Row 2: With color B, work lps off hook, **do not turn**.

Row 3: Sk first vertical bar, **sl through st** *(see Special Stitch)* across, turn.

Row 4: With color A, work lps off hook, **do not turn**.

Row 5: Sk first vertical bar, pull up lp in next vertical bar, sl through st across to last vertical bar, pull up lp in last vertical bar, turn.

Rows 6–36: [Rep rows 2–5 consecutively] 8 times, ending last rep with row 4.

Row 37: Ch 1, sk first vertical bar, sl st in each vertical bar across. Fasten off. ■

design by Mary Middleton

MATERIALS
- Medium (worsted) weight yarn:
  1 oz/50 yds/28g 2 colors A and B
- Crochenit hook used for
  photographed block

4 MEDIUM

PATTERN NOTE
Read General Instructions on pages 5–7 before beginning pattern.

SPECIAL STITCH
Heavy shell: Pull up lp in sp below next **horizontal bar** *(see illustration)*, insert hook under next 2 vertical bars at same time, yo, pull lp through.

Horizontal Bar

INSTRUCTIONS
STITCH PATTERN
Row 1: With color A, ch 20 or even number of chs, pull up lp in 2nd ch from hook, pull up lp in each ch across, turn. *(20 lps on hook)*

Row 2: With color B, work lps off hook, **do not turn.**

Row 3: Ch 1, sk first vertical bar, **heavy shell** *(see Special Stitch)* across to last horizontal bar, pull up lp in sp under last horizontal bar, turn.

Row 4: With color A, work lps off hook, **do not turn.**

Row 5: Rep row 3.

Rows 6–48: [Rep rows 2–5 consecutively] 11 times, ending last rep with row 4.

Row 49: Ch 1, sk first vertical bar, [sl st in sp under next horizontal bar, insert hook in next 2 vertical bars at same time, pull through bars and through lp on hook] across to last horizontal bar, sl st in sp under last horizontal bar. Fasten off. ■

design by Mary Middleton

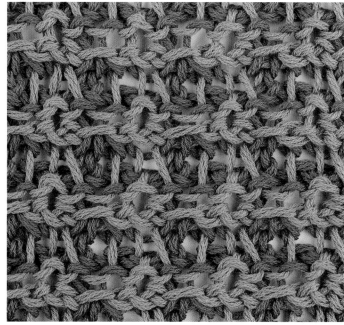

MATERIALS

- Medium (worsted) weight yarn:
  1 oz/50 yds/28g 2 colors A and B
- Crochenit hook used for
  photographed block

4 MEDIUM

PATTERN NOTE

Read General Instructions on pages 5–7 before beginning pattern.

INSTRUCTIONS

STITCH PATTERN

Row 1: With color A, ch 19 or in multiples of 3 plus 1, pull up lp in 2nd ch from hook, pull up lp in each ch across, turn. *(19 lps on hook)*

Row 2: With color B, pull through 1 lp on hook, *ch 2, yo, pull through 4 lps on hook *(this completes a ch-3 and a shell)*, rep from * across, **do not turn**.

Row 3: Ch 1, pull up lp in 3rd vertical bar of first shell, pull up lp in center ch of next ch-3, [pull up lp in first vertical bar of next shell, pull up lp in 3rd vertical bar of same shell, pull up lp in center ch of next ch-3] across to last vertical bar, pull up lp in last vertical bar, **do not turn**.

Row 4: With color A, yo, pull through 1 lp on hook, *ch 2, yo, pull through 4 lps on hook *(this completes a ch-3 and a shell)*, rep from * across, **do not turn**.

Row 5: Rep row 3.

Rows 6–48: [Rep rows 2–5 consecutively] 11 times, ending last rep with row 4.

Row 49: Ch 1, sl st in 3rd vertical bar of first shell, sl st in center ch of next ch-3, [sl st in first vertical bar of next shell, sl st in 3rd vertical bar of same shell, sl st in center ch of next ch-3] across to last vertical bar, sl st in last vertical bar. Fasten off. ■

number 17

design by Eleanor Albano Miles

MATERIALS
- Medium (worsted) weight yarn:
  1 oz/50 yds/28g 3 colors *(A, B, & C)*
- Size H/8/5mm double-ended hook used
  for photographed block

4 MEDIUM

PATTERN NOTES
Read General Instructions on pages 5–7 before beginning pattern.

Chain-4 at beginning of row or round counts as first treble crochet unless otherwise stated.

SPECIAL STITCH
Treble loop (tr lp): Yo twice, insert hook in next vertical bar or around post of next tr lp on row before last, yo, pull lp through, [yo, pull through 2 lps on hook] twice.

INSTRUCTIONS
STITCH PATTERN
Row 1: With A, ch 40 or in multiples of 21 plus 19, pull up lp in 2nd ch from hook and in each ch across, **do not turn.** *(40 lps on hook)*

Row 2: Work lps off hook, **do not turn.**

Row 3: Ch 4 *(see Pattern Notes)*, **tr lp** *(see Special Stitch)* in each of next 8 vertical bars, 3 tr lps in next vertical bar, tr lp in each of next 9 vertical bars, [sk next 2 vertical bars, tr lp in each of next 9 vertical bars, 3 tr lps in next vertical bar, tr lp in each of next 9 vertical bars] across, turn.

Row 4: With B, pull through 1 lp on hook, *[yo, pull through 2 lps on hook]** 19 times, yo, pull through 3 lps on hook, rep from * across, ending last rep at **, **do not turn**.

Row 5: Working this row around post of tr lps on row before last, ch 4, tr lp around 3rd st on row before last, tr around each of next 7 sts, [3 tr lps around next st, tr lp around each of next 9 sts, sk next 2 sts, tr lp around each of next 9 sts] across to last 11 sts, 3 tr lps around next st, tr lp around each of next 8 sts, tr lp around rem sts at same time, turn.

Next rows: Working in color sequence of A, C, A, B, rep rows 4 and 5 alternately. At end of last row, fasten off. ■

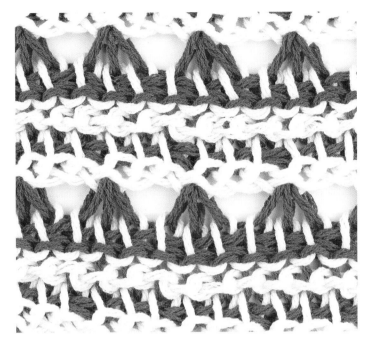

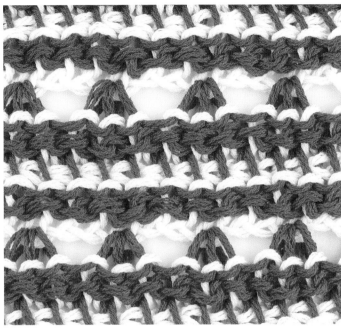

MATERIALS
- Medium (worsted) weight yarn:
  1 oz/50 yds/28g 2 colors A and B
- Crochenit hook used for
  photographed block

4 MEDIUM

PATTERN NOTE
Read General Instructions on pages 5–7 before beginning pattern.

INSTRUCTIONS
STITCH PATTERN
Row 1: With color A, ch 19 or in multiples of 3 plus 1 chs, pull up lp in 2nd ch from hook, pull up lp in each ch across, turn. *(19 lps on hook)*

Row 2: With color B, work lps off hook, **do not turn**.

Row 3: Sk first vertical bar, pull up lp in 2nd vertical bar, pull up lp in each vertical bar across, turn.

Row 4: With color A, work lps off hook, **do not turn**.

Row 5: Rep row 3.

Row 6: With color B, work lps off hook, **do not turn**.

Row 7: Rep row 3.

Row 8: With color A, pull through first lp on hook, *ch 2, yo, pull through 4 lps on hook *(this completes a ch-3 and a shell)*, rep from * across, **do not turn**.

Row 9: Ch 1, sk shells, pull up lp in top lp of each ch across, turn. *(19 lps on hook)*

Rows 10–36: [Rep rows 2–9 consecutively] 4 times, ending last rep with row 4.

Row 37: Sk first vertical bar, sl st in each vertical bar across. Fasten off. ∎

design by Jennifer McClain

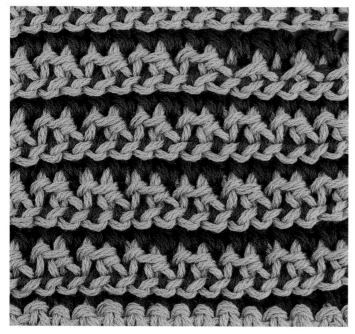

MATERIALS
- Medium (worsted) weight yarn:
  1 oz/50 yds/28g 2 colors A and B
- Size H/8/5mm double-ended hook used
  for photographed block

4 MEDIUM

PATTERN NOTE
Read General Instructions on pages 5–7 before beginning pattern.

SPECIAL STITCHES
Single crochet loop (sc lp): Insert hook in next ch or vertical bar, yo, pull lp through, yo, pull through 1 lp on hook.

Post double crochet loop (pdc lp): Yo, insert hook around both strands of next vertical bar from right to left, yo, pull lp through, yo, pull though 2 lps on hook.

INSTRUCTIONS
STITCH PATTERN
Row 1: With color A, ch 20 or even number of ch, **sc lp** (see Special Stitches) in 3rd ch from hook, sc lp in each ch across, turn. (19 lps on hook)

Row 2: With color B, work lps off hook, **do not turn**.

Row 3: Ch 1, ***pdc lp** (see Special Stitches), sc lp, rep from * across, turn.

Row 4: With color A, work lps off hook, **do not turn**.

Row 5: Rep row 3.

Rows 6–24: [Rep rows 2–5 consecutively] 5 times, ending last rep with row 4.

Row 25: Ch 1, sc around first vertical bar, [dc around both strands of next vertical bar, sc around front lp of next vertical bar] across. Fasten off. ■

number 20

design by Jennifer McClain

MATERIALS
- Medium (worsted) weight yarn:
  1 oz/50 yds/28g 2 colors A and B
- Size H/8/5mm double-ended hook used
  for photographed block

4 MEDIUM

PATTERN NOTE
Read General Instructions on pages 5–7 before beginning pattern.

SPECIAL STITCH
Single crochet loop (sc lp): Insert hook in next ch or vertical bar, yo, pull lp through, yo, pull through 1 lp on hook.

INSTRUCTIONS
STITCH PATTERN
Row 1: With color A, ch 20 or even number of chs, **sc lp** (see Special Stitch) in 3rd ch from hook, sc lp in each ch across, turn. (19 lps on hook)

Row 2: With color B, work lps off hook, **do not turn**.

Row 3: Ch 1, pull up lp in top strand of first **horizontal bar** (see illustration), insert hook under next 2 vertical bars at same time, yo, pull lp through, ch 1, [pull up lp in top strand of next horizontal bar, insert hook under next 2 vertical bars at same time, yo, pull lp through, ch 1] across to last vertical bar, pull up lp in last vertical bar, turn.

Horizontal Bar

Row 4: With color A, work lps off hook, **do not turn**.

Row 5: Rep row 3.

Rows 6–22: [Rep rows 2–5 consecutively] 5 times, ending last rep with row 2.

Row 23: Ch 1, sc in each vertical bar across. Fasten off. ■

design by Jennifer McClain

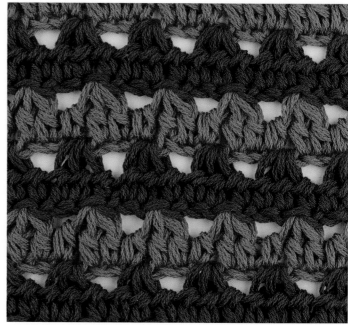

MATERIALS
- Medium (worsted) weight yarn:
  1 oz/50 yds/28g 2 colors A and B
- Size H/8/5mm double-ended hook used
  for photographed block

4 MEDIUM

PATTERN NOTE
Read General Instructions on pages 5–7 before beginning pattern.

SPECIAL STITCH
Double crochet loop (dc lp): Yo, insert hook in place indicated, yo, pull lp through, yo, pull through 2 lps on hook.

INSTRUCTIONS
STITCH PATTERN
Row 1: With color A, ch 21 or in multiples of 3 chs, **dc lp** *(see Special Stitch)* in 3rd ch from hook, dc lp in each ch across, turn. *(20 lps on hook)*

Row 2: With color B, pull through first lp on hook, ch 1, yo, pull through 4 lps on hook *(completes a ch-2 and a shell)* *ch 2, yo, pull through 4 lps on hook *(completes a ch-3 and a shell)*, rep from * across to last 2 lps on hook, ch 1, yo, pull through last 2 lps *(completes a ch-2 and a vertical bar)*, **do not turn**.

Row 3: Ch 1, sk all shells, dc lp in each ch across, turn. *(20 lps on hook)*

Rows 4 & 5: With color A, rep rows 2 and 3.

Rows 6–14: [Rep rows 2–5 consecutively] 3 times, ending last rep with row 2.

Row 15: Ch 2, sk all shells, hdc in each ch across. Fasten off. ■

design by Jennifer McClain

MATERIALS
- Medium (worsted) weight yarn:
  1 oz/50 yds/28g 2 colors A and B
- Size H/8/5mm double-ended hook used
  for photographed block

4 MEDIUM

PATTERN NOTE
Read General Instructions on pages 5–7 before
beginning pattern.

SPECIAL STITCHES
Single crochet loop (sc lp): Insert hook in next ch or
vertical bar, yo, pull lp through, yo, pull through 1 lp
on hook.

Double crochet loop (dc lp): Yo, insert hook in place
indicated, yo, pull lp through, yo, pull through 2 lps
on hook.

INSTRUCTIONS
STITCH PATTERN
Row 1: With color A, ch 20 or even number of chs,
sc lp *(see Special Stitches)* in 3rd ch from hook, sc lp
in each ch across, turn. *(19 lps on hook)*

Row 2: With color B, work lps off hook, **do not turn**.

Row 3: Ch 1, ***dc lp** *(see Special Stitches)* in next
vertical bar, sc lp in next vertical bar, rep from *
across, turn.

Row 4: With color A, work lps off hook, **do not turn**.

Row 5: Rep row 3.

Rows 6–16: [Rep rows 2–5 consecutively] 3 times,
ending last rep with row 4.

Row 17: Ch 2, hdc in each vertical bar across.
Fasten off. ∎

design by Jennifer McClain

MATERIALS

- Medium (worsted) weight yarn:
  1 oz/50 yds/28g 2 colors A and B
- Size H/8/5mm double-ended hook used
  for photographed block

4 MEDIUM

PATTERN NOTE

Read General Instructions on pages 5–7 before beginning pattern.

INSTRUCTIONS

STITCH PATTERN

Row 1: With color A, ch 20 or desired number of chs, pull up lp in 2nd ch from hook, pull up lp in each ch across, turn. *(20 lps on hook)*

Row 2: With color B, work lps off hook, **do not turn**.

Row 3: Ch 1, pull up lp in top strand of each **horizontal bar** *(see illustration)* across, turn.

Horizontal Bar

Rows 4 & 5: With color A, rep rows 2 and 3.

Rows 6–28: [Rep rows 2–5 consecutively] 6 times, ending last rep with row 4.

Row 29: Ch 1, sc in each horizontal bar across. Fasten off. ■

design by Darla Fanton

MATERIALS

- Medium (worsted) weight yarn:
  1 oz/50 yds/28g 2 colors A and B
- Size H/8/5mm double-ended hook used
  for photographed block

4 MEDIUM

PATTERN NOTE

Read General Instructions on pages 5–7 before beginning pattern.

INSTRUCTIONS

STITCH PATTERN

Row 1: With color A, ch 50 or in multiples of 50 chs, pull up lp in 2nd ch from hook, pull up lp in each ch across, turn. *(50 lps on hook)*

Row 2: With color B, work lps off hook, **do not turn.**

Row 3: Sk first **horizontal bar** *(see illustration)*, pull up lp in top strand of each of next 10 horizontal bars, *pull up lp in next vertical bar, pull up lp in top strand of next horizontal bar, pull up lp in next vertical bar**, pull up lp in top strand of each of next 11 horizontal bars, sk next 2 horizontal

Horizontal Bar

bars, pull up lp in top strand of each of next 11 horizontal bars, if working with more than 50 sts, rep between from * across to last 10 horizontal bars, ending last rep at **, pull up lp in top strand of each of next 10 horizontal bars, sk next horizontal bar, pull up lp in top strand of last horizontal bar, turn.

Row 4: With color A, work lps off hook, **do not turn.**

Row 5: Rep row 3.

Rows 6–24: [Rep rows 2–5 consecutively] 5 times, ending last rep with row 4.

Row 25: Sk first horizontal bar, sl st in top strand of each of next 10 horizontal bars, *sl st in top strand of next vertical bar, sl st in top strand of next horizontal bar, sl st in next vertical bar**, sl st in top strand of each of next 11 horizontal bars, sk next 2 horizontal bars, pull up lp in top strand of each of next 11 horizontal bars, if working with more than 50 sts, rep from * across to last 10 horizontal bars, ending last rep at **, pull up lp in top strand of each of next 10 horizontal bars, sk next horizontal bar, pull up lp in top strand of last horizontal bar. Fasten off. ■

design by Jennifer McClain

MATERIALS
- Medium (worsted) weight yarn:
  1 oz/50 yds/28g 2 colors A and B
- Size H/8/5mm double-ended hook used
  for photographed block

4 MEDIUM

PATTERN NOTE
Read General Instructions on pages 5–7 before beginning pattern.

SPECIAL STITCH
Single crochet loop (sc lp): Insert hook in next ch or vertical bar, yo, pull lp through, yo, pull through 1 lp on hook.

INSTRUCTIONS

STITCH PATTERN
Row 1: With color A, ch 21 or desired number of chs, **sc lp** *(see Special Stitch)* in 3rd ch from hook, sc lp in each ch across, turn. *(20 lps on hook)*

Row 2: With color B, work lps off hook, **do not turn**.

Row 3: Ch 1, sk first vertical bar, sc lp in each vertical bar across, turn.

Rows 4 & 5: With color A, rep rows 2 and 3.

Rows 6–20: [Rep rows 2–5 consecutively] 4 times, ending last rep with row 4.

Row 21: Ch 1, sk first vertical bar, sc in each vertical bar across. Fasten off. ■

design by Ann Parnell

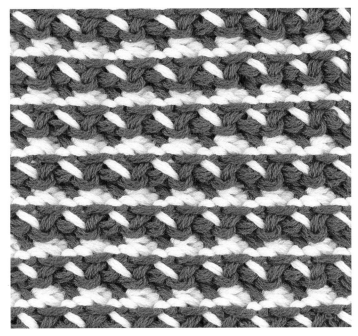

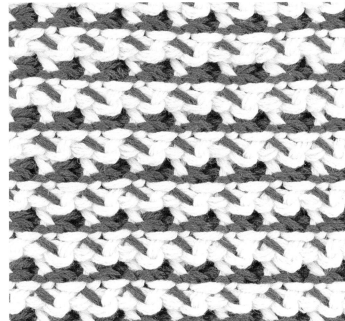

MATERIALS

- Medium (worsted) weight yarn:
  1 oz/50 yds/28g 2 colors A and B
- H/8/5mm double-ended hook used for photographed block

4

MEDIUM

PATTERN NOTE

Read General Instructions on pages 5–7 before beginning pattern.

SPECIAL STITCH

Cross-stitch (cross-st): Sk next vertical bar, pull up lp in next vertical bar, pull up lp in sk vertical bar.

INSTRUCTIONS

STITCH PATTERN

Row 1: With color A, ch 20 or even number of chs, pull up lp in 2nd ch from hook, pull up lp in each ch across, turn. *(20 lps on hook)*

Row 2: With color B, work lps off hook, **do not turn**.

Row 3: Sk first vertical bar, **cross-st** *(see Special Stitch)* across to last vertical bar, pull up lp in last vertical bar, turn.

Rows 4 & 5: With color A, rep rows 2 and 3.

Rows 6–32: [Rep rows 2–5 consecutively] 7 times, ending last rep with row 4.

Row 33: Ch 1, sk first vertical bar, sc in each vertical bar across. Fasten off. ■

design by Darla Fanton

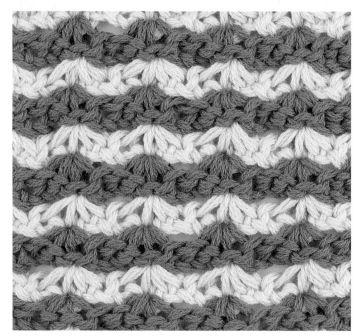

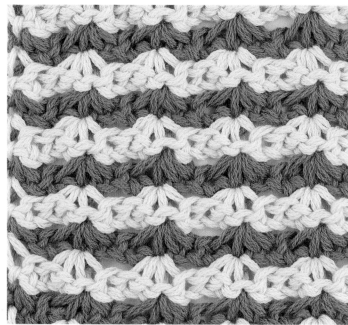

MATERIALS
- Medium (worsted) weight yarn:
  1 oz/50 yds/28g 2 colors A and B
- Size H/8/5mm double-ended hook used
  for photographed block

4 MEDIUM

PATTERN NOTE
Read General Instructions on pages 5–7 before beginning pattern.

SPECIAL STITCHES
Beginning shell (beg shell): Yo, pull through first 2 lps on hook.

Shell: Yo, pull through 5 lps on hook.

End shell: Yo, pull through last 4 lps on hook.

INSTRUCTIONS
STITCH PATTERN
Row 1: With color A, ch 21 or multiples of 4 plus 5 chs, pull up lp in 2nd ch from hook, pull up lp in each ch across, turn. *(21 lps on hook)*

Row 2: With color B, **beg shell** *(see Special Stitches)*, ch 3, [**shell** *(see Special Stitches)*, ch 3] across to last 4 lps on hook, **end shell** *(see Special Stitches)*, **do not turn.**

Row 3: Sk first shell, pull up lp in each of next 3 chs, [pull up lp in next shell, pull up lp in each of next 3 chs] across to last shell, pull up lp in last shell, turn.

Rows 4 & 5: With color A, rep rows 2 and 3.

Rows 6–21: [Rep rows 2–5 consecutively] 4 times.

Row 22: With color B, beg shell, ch 2, [shell, ch 2] across to last 4 lps on hook, end shell. Fasten off. ■

design by Ann Parnell

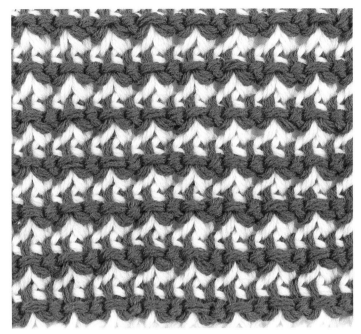

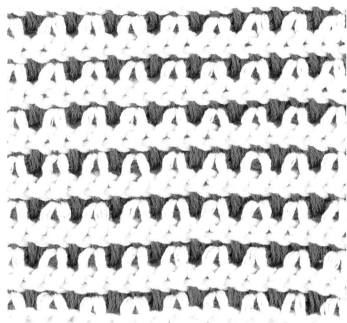

MATERIALS

- Medium (worsted) weight yarn:
  1 oz/50 yds/28g 2 colors A and B
- H/8/5mm double-ended hook used for
  photographed block

4 MEDIUM

PATTERN NOTE

Read General Instructions on pages 5–7 before
beginning pattern.

INSTRUCTIONS

STITCH PATTERN

Row 1: With color A, ch 24 or even number of chs,
pull up lp in 2nd ch from hook, pull up lp in each ch
across, turn. *(24 lps on hook)*

Row 2: With color B, pull through first 2 lps on hook,
*ch 1, yo, pull through 3 lps on hook *(completes a
ch-1 and a shell)*, rep from * across to last 2 lps on

hook, ch 1, yo, pull through last 2 lps on hook,
do not turn.

Row 3: Ch 1, pull up lp in each ch-1 and
in each **horizontal bar** *(see illustration)*
at top of each shell across, turn.
(24 lps on hook)

Horizontal Bar

Row 4: With color A, work lps off hook, **do not turn**.

Row 5: Ch 1, pull up lp in top strand of each
horizontal bar across, turn.

Rows 6–30: [Rep rows 2–5 consecutively] 7 times,
ending last rep with row 2.

Row 31: Ch 1, sl st in each ch-1 and in each
horizontal bar at top of each shell across. Fasten off. ■

number 29

design by Ann Parnell

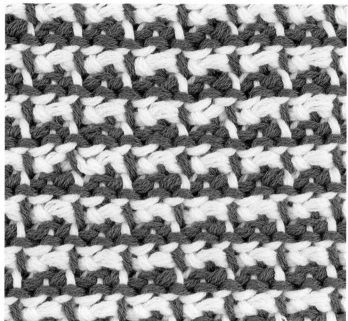

MATERIALS
- Medium (worsted) weight yarn:
    1 oz/50 yds/28g 2 colors A and B
- H/8/5mm double-ended hook used for
  photographed block

4 MEDIUM

PATTERN NOTE
Read General Instructions on pages 5–7 before beginning pattern.

INSTRUCTIONS
STITCH PATTERN
Row 1: With color A, ch 22 or even number of chs, pull up lp in 2nd ch from hook, pull up lp in each ch across, turn. *(22 lps on hook)*

Row 2: With color B, work lps off hook, **do not turn**.

Row 3: Sk first vertical bar, pull up lp in next vertical bar; *holding yarn in front of work, pull up lp in next vertical bar; holding yarn in back of work, pull up lp in next vertical bar, rep from * across, turn.

Row 4: With color A, work lps off hook, **do not turn**.

Row 5: Rep row 3.

Rows 6–32: [Rep rows 2–5 consecutively] 7 times, ending last rep with row 4.

Row 33: Ch 1, sl st in each vertical bar across. Fasten off. ■

design by Ann Parnell

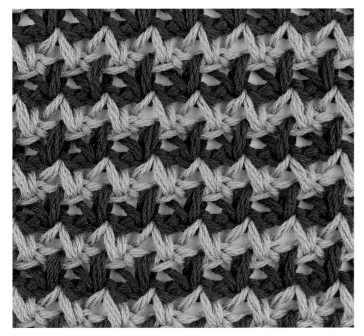

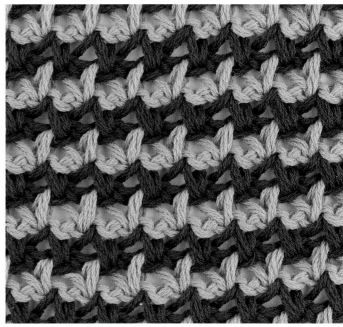

MATERIALS

- Medium (worsted) weight yarn:
  1 oz/50 yds/28g 2 colors A and B
- H/8/5mm double-ended hook used for photographed block

PATTERN NOTE

Read General Instructions on pages 5–7 before beginning pattern.

INSTRUCTIONS

STITCH PATTERN

Row 1: With color A, ch 23 or in multiples of 2 plus 1 chs, pull up lp in 2nd ch from hook, pull up lp in each ch across, turn. *(23 lps on hook)*

Row 2: With color B, pull through first lp on hook, [ch 1, yo, pull through 3 lps on hook] across, **do not turn.**

Row 3: Pull up lp under top 2 lps of next ch-1, [yo, sk next 2 vertical bars, pull up lp under top 2 lps of next ch-1] across to last vertical bar, pull up lp in last vertical bar, turn. *(23 lps on hook)*

Row 4: With color A, work lps off hook, **do not turn.**

Row 5: Rep row 3.

Rows 6–32: [Rep rows 2–5 consecutively] 7 times, ending last rep with row 4.

Row 33: Ch 1, sl st in each vertical bar across. Fasten off. ■

design by Ann Parnell

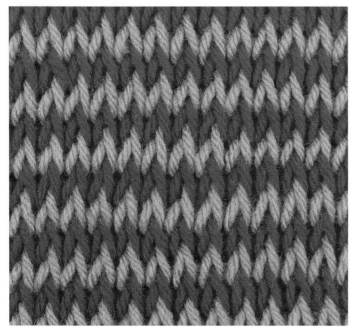

MATERIALS

- Medium (worsted) weight yarn:
  1 oz/50 yds/28g 2 colors A and B
- K/10½/6.5mm double-ended hook used
  for photographed block

4
MEDIUM

PATTERN NOTE

Read General Instructions on pages 5–7 before beginning pattern.

SPECIAL STITCHES

Knit: Insert hook between front and back vertical bars *(see illustration)* and under horizontal bar of next st, yo, pull up lp.

Knit Stitch

Purl: Holding yarn to front of work and hook at back of work, insert hook from back to front through back and front vertical bars of next st, yo, pull up lp.

INSTRUCTIONS

STITCH PATTERN

Row 1: With color A, ch 20 or desired number of chs, pull up lp in 2nd ch from hook, pull up lp in each ch across, turn. *(20 lps on hook)*

Row 2: With color B, work lps off hook, **do not turn**.

Row 3: Sk first vertical bar, **knit** *(see Special Stitches)* across to last vertical bar; for last st, insert hook between first and back vertical bars of last st, yo, pull up lp, turn.

Row 4: With color A, work lps off hook, **do not turn**.

Row 5: Sk first vertical bar, **purl** *(see Special Stitches)* across, turn.

Rows 6–38: [Rep rows 2–5 consecutively] 9 times, ending last rep with row 2.

Row 39: Sl st in each vertical bar across. Fasten off. ■

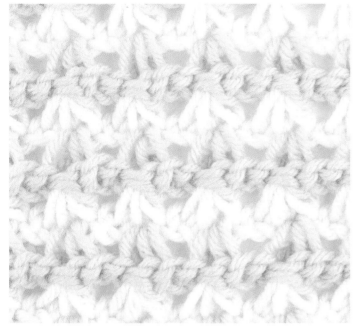

MATERIALS
- Medium (worsted) weight yarn:
  1 oz/50 yds/28g 2 colors A and B
- K/10½/6.5mm double-ended hook used
  for photographed block

PATTERN NOTE
Read General Instructions on pages 5–7 before
beginning pattern.

INSTRUCTIONS
STITCH PATTERN
Row 1: With color A, ch 26 or in multiples of 3 plus 2
chs, pull up lp in 2nd ch from hook, pull up lp in each
ch across, turn. *(26 lps on hook)*

Row 2: With color B, pull through first lp on hook, ch
1, yo, pull through 4 lps on hook *(completes a ch-2*

and a shell), *ch 2, yo, pull through 4 lps on hook
(completes a ch-3 and a shell), rep from * across to
last 2 lps on hook, ch 1, yo, pull through last 2 lps
on hook, *(completes a ch-2 and a vertical bar)*,
do not turn.

Row 3: Pull up lp in each ch across, turn.
(26 lps on hook)

Row 4: With color A, rep row 2.

Row 5: Pull up lp in each ch across, turn.
(26 lps on hook)

Rows 6–26: [Rep rows 2–5 consecutively] 6 times,
ending last rep with row 2.

Row 27: Sl st in each ch across. Fasten off. ■

design by Mary Middleton

MATERIALS

- Medium (worsted) weight yarn:
  1 oz/50 yds/28g 2 colors A and B
- Crochenit hook used for
  photographed block

4 MEDIUM

PATTERN NOTE

Read General Instructions on pages 5–7 before beginning pattern.

INSTRUCTIONS

STITCH PATTERN

Row 1: With color A, ch 22 or in multiples of 3 plus 1 chs, pull up lp in 2nd ch from hook, pull up lp in each ch across, turn. *(22 lps on hook)*

Row 2: With color B, pull through first lp on hook, *ch 2, yo, pull through 4 lps on hook *(completes a ch-3 and a shell—see photo)*, rep from * across, **do not turn**.

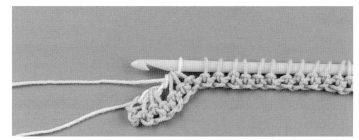

Row 3: Ch 1, sk all shells, pull up lp in top strand of each ch across, turn. *(22 lps on hook)*

Rows 4 & 5: With color A, rep rows 2 and 3.

Rows 6–28: [Rep rows 2–5 consecutively] 6 times, ending last rep with row 4.

Row 29: Ch 1, sk all shells, sl st in each ch across. Fasten off. ■

design by Mary Middleton

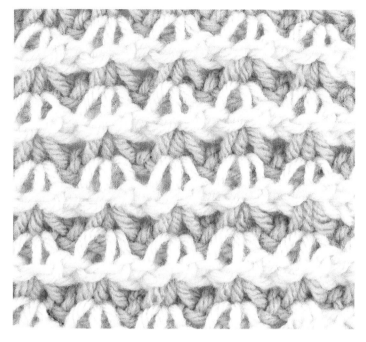

MATERIALS

- Medium (worsted) weight yarn:
  1 oz/50 yds/28g 2 colors A and B
- Crochenit hook used for
  photographed block

4 MEDIUM

PATTERN NOTE

Read General Instructions on pages 5–7 before beginning pattern.

INSTRUCTIONS

STITCH PATTERN

Row 1: With color A, ch 19 or in multiples of 3 plus 1 chs, pull up lp in 2nd ch from hook, pull up lp in each ch across, turn. *(19 lps on hook)*

Row 2: With color B, pull through first 2 lps on hook *(completes a shell)*, *ch 1, yo, pull through 4 lps on

hook *(completes a ch-2 and a shell)*, rep from * across to last 3 lps on hook, ch 1, yo, pull through last 3 lps on hook *(completes a ch-2 and a shell)*, **do not turn.**

Row 3: Ch 1, sk first shell, pull up lp in each ch-1 and in each **horizontal bar** *(see illustration)* at top of each shell across, turn. *(19 lps on hook)*

Horizontal Bar

Rows 4 & 5: With color A, rep rows 2 and 3.

Rows 6–24: [Rep rows 2–5 consecutively] 5 times, ending last rep with row 4.

Row 25: Ch 1, sl st in each ch and in each horizontal bar at top of each shell across to last vertical bar, sl st in last vertical bar. Fasten off. ∎

design by Mary Middleton

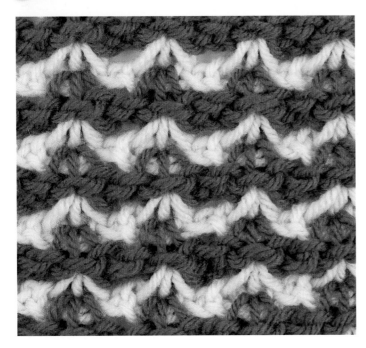

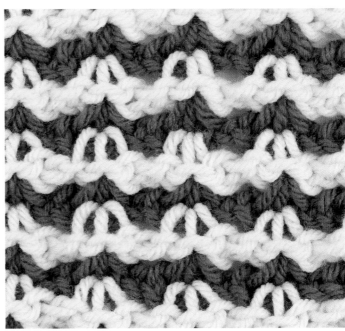

MATERIALS
- Medium (worsted) weight yarn:
  1 oz/50 yds/28g 2 colors A and B
- Crochenit hook used for
  photographed block

4 MEDIUM

PATTERN NOTE
Read General Instructions on pages 5–7 before beginning pattern.

INSTRUCTIONS
STITCH PATTERN
Row 1: With color A, ch 19 or in multiples of 3 plus 1 chs, pull up lp in 2nd ch from hook, pull up lp in each ch across, turn. *(19 lps on hook)*

Row 2: With color B, pull through first 2 lps on hook *(completes a shell)*, *ch 2, yo, pull through 4 lps on hook *(completes a ch-3 and a shell)*, rep from * across to last 3 lps on hook, ch 2, yo, pull through last 3 lps on hook *(completes a ch-3 and a shell)*, **do not turn.**

Row 3: Ch 1, [pull up a lp in first ch of next ch-3, pull up a lp in 3rd ch of same ch-3, pull up a lp in next **horizontal bar** *(see illustration)* at top of next shell] across, turn.

Horizontal Bar

Rows 4 & 5: With color A, rep rows 2 and 3.

Rows 6–28: [Rep rows 2–5 consecutively] 6 times, ending last rep with row 4.

Row 29: Ch 1, sk first shell, sl st in first and last ch of each ch-3 and in each horizontal bar at top of each shell across. Fasten off. ■

design by Mary Middleton

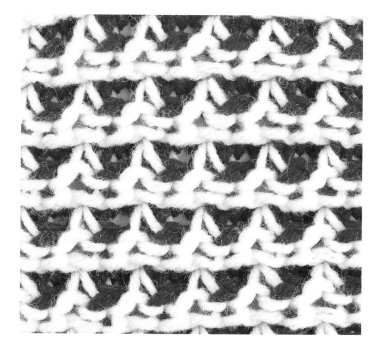

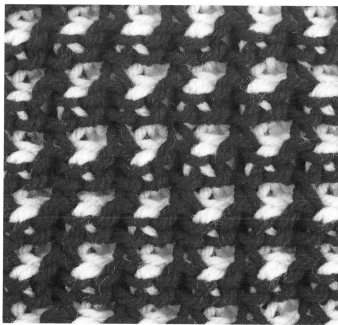

MATERIALS

- Medium (worsted) weight yarn:
  1 oz/50 yds/28g 2 colors A and B
- Crochenit hook used for
  photographed block

4 MEDIUM

PATTERN NOTE

Read General Instructions on pages 5–7 before beginning pattern.

INSTRUCTIONS

STITCH PATTERN

Row 1: With color A, ch 18 or even number of chs, pull up lp in 2nd ch from hook, pull up lp in each ch across, turn. *(18 lps on hook)*

Row 2: With color B, work lps off hook, **do not turn**.

Row 3: Ch 1, pull up lp in top strand of first **horizontal bar** *(see illustration)*, insert hook under next 2 vertical bars at same time, yo, pull up lp, [pull up lp in top strand of next horizontal bar, insert hook under next 2 vertical bars at same time, yo, pull up lp] across to last horizontal bar, pull up lp in top strand of last horizontal bar, turn.

Horizontal Bar

Rows 4 & 5: With color A, rep rows 2 and 3.

Rows 6–32: [Rep rows 2–5 consecutively] 7 times, ending last rep with row 4.

Row 33: Ch 1, sl st in top strand of first horizontal bar, sl st in next 2 vertical bars at same time, [sl st in top strand of next horizontal bar, sl st in next 2 vertical bars at same time] across to last horizontal bar, sl st in top strand of last horizontal bar. Fasten off. ■

design by Mary Middleton

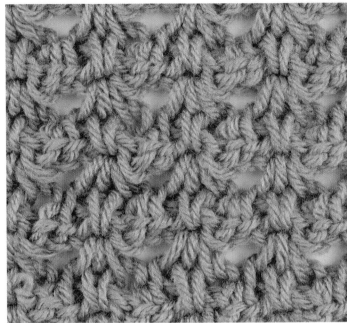

MATERIALS

- Medium (worsted) weight yarn:
  1 oz/50 yds/28g 2 colors A and B
- Crochenit hook used for
  photographed block

4 MEDIUM

PATTERN NOTE

Read General Instructions on pages 5–7 before beginning pattern.

SPECIAL STITCH

Single crochet loop (sc lp): Insert hook in place indicated, yo, pull up lp, ch 1.

INSTRUCTIONS

STITCH PATTERN

Row 1: With color A, ch 19 or multiples of 3 plus 1 chs, **sc lp** (see Special Stitch) in 3rd ch from hook, sc lp in each ch across, turn. (19 lps on hook)

Row 2: With color B, pull through first lp on hook, *ch 2, yo, pull through 4 lps on hook (this completes a ch-3 and a shell), rep from * across, **do not turn**.

Row 3: Ch 1, *sk next shell, pull up lp in first ch of next ch-3, insert hook in ch directly below on row 1, yo, pull lp through, ch 1, pull up lp in last ch of same ch-3 (this completes a corn st), rep from * across, turn.

Row 4: With color A, pull through first lp on hook, *ch 2, yo, pull through 4 lps on hook (this completes a ch-3 and a shell), rep from * across, **do not turn**.

Row 5: Ch 1, *sk next shell, pull up lp in first ch of next ch-3, insert hook under 2 **horizontal bars** (see illustration) above next shell 3 rows below, yo, pull lp through, ch 1, pull up lp in last ch of same ch-3 (this completes a corn st), rep from * across, turn.

Horizontal Bar

Rows 6 & 7: With color B, rep rows 4 and 5.

Rows 8–24: [Rep rows 4–7 consecutively] 5 times, ending last rep with row 4.

Row 25: Ch 1, sl st in each ch across. Fasten off. ■

design by Dorris Brooks

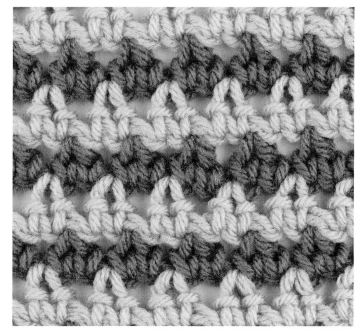

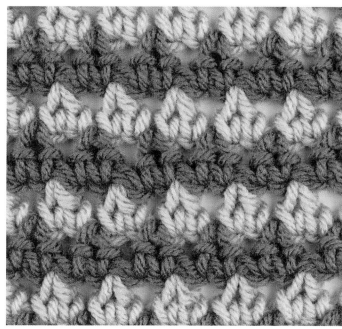

MATERIALS

- Medium (worsted) weight yarn:
  1 oz/50 yds/28g 2 colors A and B
- K/10½/6.5mm double-ended hook used
  for photographed block

4 MEDIUM

PATTERN NOTE

Read General Instructions on pages 5–7 before beginning pattern.

SPECIAL STITCH

Single crochet loop (sc lp): Pull up lp in place indicated, ch 1.

INSTRUCTIONS

STITCH PATTERN

Row 1: With color A, ch 20 or even number of chs, **sc lp** (see Special Stitch) in 2nd ch from hook, sc lp in each ch across, turn. (20 lps on hook)

Row 2: With color B, pull through first lp on hook, yo, pull through 3 lps on hook (completes a shell), *ch 1,

yo, pull through 3 lps on hook (completes a ch-2 and a shell), rep from * across to last 2 lps on hook, ch 1, yo, pull through last 2 lps on hook (completes a ch-2 and a vertical bar), **do not turn**.

Row 3: Ch 1, sk first vertical bar, sc lp in next 2 chs, [sk next shell, sc lp in next 2 chs] across to last shell, sk last shell, sc lp under top 2 strands of last **horizontal bar** (see illustration), turn.

Horizontal Bar

Rows 4 & 5: With color A, rep rows 2 and 3.

Rows 6–24: [Rep rows 2–5 consecutively] 5 times, ending last rep with row 4.

Row 25: Ch 1, sc in each ch across to last horizontal bar, sc under top 2 strands of last horizontal bar. Fasten off. ■

design by Dorris Brooks

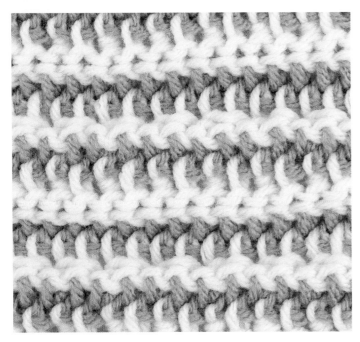

MATERIALS
- Medium (worsted) weight yarn:
  1 oz/50 yds/28g 2 colors A and B
- K/10½/6.5mm double-ended hook used
  for photographed block

PATTERN NOTE
Read General Instructions on pages 5–7 before beginning pattern.

SPECIAL STITCH
Post stitch (post st): Yo, insert hook around both strands of indicated vertical bar 4 rows below, yo, pull lp through, yo, pull through 2 lps on hook, ch 1, sk horizontal bar on last row behind post st.

INSTRUCTIONS
STITCH PATTERN
Row 1: With color A, ch 21 or odd number of chs, pull up lp in 2nd ch from hook, pull up lp in each ch across, turn. *(21 lps on hook)*

Row 2: With color B, work lps off hook, **do not turn**.

Row 3: Ch 1, pull up lp in top strand of each **horizontal bar** *(see illustration)* across, turn.

Horizontal Bar

Row 4: With color A, work lps off hook, **do not turn**.

Row 5: Ch 1, pull up lp in top strand of each horizontal bar across, turn.

Row 6: With color B, work lps off hook, **do not turn**.

Row 7: Ch 1, pull up lp in first horizontal bar, ***post st** *(see Special Stitch)* around 3rd vertical bar 4 rows below, [pull up lp in next horizontal bar on last row, sk next vertical bar 4 rows below, post st around next vertical bar 4 rows below] across to last 2 horizontal bars on last row, pull up lp in last 2 horizontal bars, turn.

Rows 8–24: [Rep rows 4–7 consecutively] 5 times, ending last rep with row 4.

Row 25: Ch 1, sl st in each vertical bar across. Fasten off. ■

design by Dorris Brooks

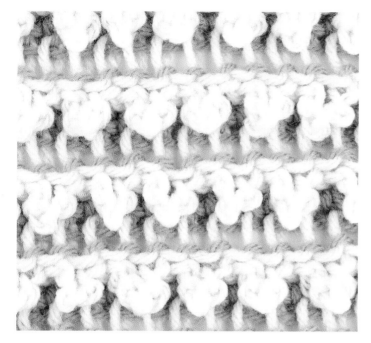

MATERIALS
- Medium (worsted) weight yarn:
  1 oz/50 yds/28g 2 colors A and B
- K/10½/6.5mm double-ended hook
  used for photographed block

PATTERN NOTE
Read General Instructions on pages 5–7 before beginning pattern.

SPECIAL STITCH
Single crochet loop (sc lp): Insert hook in place indicated, yo, pull up lp, ch 1.

INSTRUCTIONS
STITCH PATTERN
Row 1: With color A, ch 20 or even number of chs, **sc lp** (see Special Stitch) in 2nd ch from hook, sc lp in each ch across, turn. *(20 lps on hook)*

Row 2: With color B, pull through first lp on hook, yo, pull through 2 lps on hook, [ch 4, pull last ch through 1 lp on hook, yo, pull through 2 lps on hook] across, turn, **do not turn**.

Row 3: Ch 1, pull up lp in each vertical bar across, turn.

Row 4: With color A, work lps off hook, **do not turn**.

Row 5: Ch 1, sc lp in each **horizontal bar** *(see illustration)* across, turn.

Horizontal Bar

Row 6: With color B, pull through first lp on hook, [yo, pull through 2 lps on hook] twice, [ch 4, pull last lp through 1 lp on hook, yo, pull through 2 lps on hook] across to last 3 lps on hook, [yo, pull through 2 lps on hook] twice, **do not turn**.

Row 7: Ch 1, pull up lp in each vertical bar across, turn.

Row 8: With color A, work lps off hook, **do not turn**.

Row 9: Ch 1, sc lp in each horizontal bar across, turn.

Rows 10–20: [Rep rows 2–9 consecutively] twice, ending last rep with row 4.

Row 21: Ch 1, sl st in each vertical bar across. Fasten off. ■

design by Mary Ann Sipes

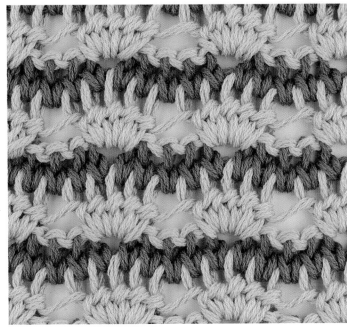

MATERIALS
- Medium (worsted) weight yarn:
  1 oz/50 yds/28g 2 colors A and B
- H/8/5mm double-ended hook used for photographed block

4 MEDIUM

PATTERN NOTE
Read General Instructions on pages 5–7 before beginning pattern.

SPECIAL STITCHES
Single crochet loop (sc lp): Insert hook in place indicated, yo, pull lp through, ch 1.

Double crochet loop (dc lp): Yo insert hook in place indicated, yo, pull lp through, yo, pull through 2 lps on hook.

Scallop: 5 dc lps under next horizontal bar.

INSTRUCTIONS
STITCH PATTERN
Row 1: With color A, ch 25 or multiples of 5 chs, pull up lp in 2nd ch from hook, pull up lp in each ch across, turn. *(25 lps on hook)*

Row 2: With color B, work lps off hook, **do not turn**.

Row 3: Ch 1, sk first vertical bar, **sc lp** *(see Special Stitches)* under each **horizontal bar** *(see illustration)* across, turn.

Horizontal Bar

Row 4: With color A, work lps off hook, **do not turn**.

Row 5: Ch 2, **dc lp** *(see Special Stitches)* in first vertical bar, sk next 4 horizontal bars *scallop (see Special Stitches)* under next horizontal bar, sk next 4 horizontal bars, rep from * across to last vertical bar, 2 dc lps in last vertical bar, turn.

Row 6: With color B, work lps off hook, **do not turn**.

Row 7: Ch 1, sk first vertical bar, sc lp under each horizontal bar across to last vertical bar, sc lp in last vertical bar, turn.

Rows 8–28: [Rep rows 4–7 consecutively] 6 times, ending last rep with row 4.

Row 29: Ch 1, sk first vertical bar, sl st in each vertical bar across. Fasten off. ∎

design by Mary Ann Sipes

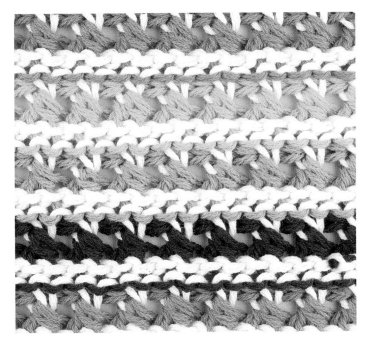

MATERIALS
- Medium (worsted) weight yarn:
  1 oz/50 yds/28g 5 colors white,
  A, B, C and D
- Size H/8/5mm double-ended hook used
  for photographed block

4 MEDIUM

PATTERN NOTE
Read General Instructions on pages 5–7 before
beginning pattern.

SPECIAL STITCHES
Double crochet loop (dc lp): Yo, insert hook in place
indicated, yo, pull lp through, yo, pull through 2 lps
on hook.

Cross-stitch (cross-st): Sk next vertical bar, dc lp in
next vertical bar, working in front of st just worked,
dc lp in sk vertical bar.

INSTRUCTIONS
STITCH PATTERN
Row 1: With white, ch 30 or even number of chs,
pull up lp in 2nd ch from hook, pull up lp in each ch
across, turn. *(30 lps on hook)*

Row 2: With color A, work lps off hook, **do not turn**.

Row 3: Ch 1, sk first vertical bar, **cross-st** *(see Special
Stitches)* across to last vertical bar, **dc lp** *(see Special
Stitches)* in last vertical bar, turn.

Row 4: With white, work lps off hook, **do not turn**.

Row 5: Ch 1, sk first vertical bar, pull up lp in each
vertical bar across, turn.

Row 6: With color B, work lps off hook, **do not turn**.

Row 7: Ch 1, sk first vertical bar, cross-st across to
last vertical bar, dc lp in last vertical bar, turn.

Rows 8–36: Working in color sequence of white,
color C, white, color D, white, color A, white, color B,
[rep rows 4–7 consecutively] 8 times, ending last rep
with row 4 and white.

Row 37: Ch 1, sk first vertical bar, sl st in each vertical
bar across. Fasten off. ■

design by Mary Ann Sipes

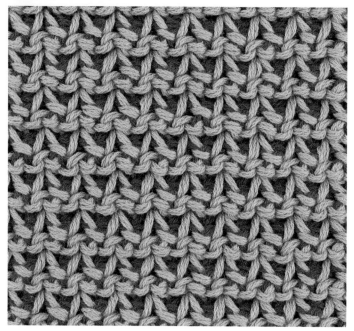

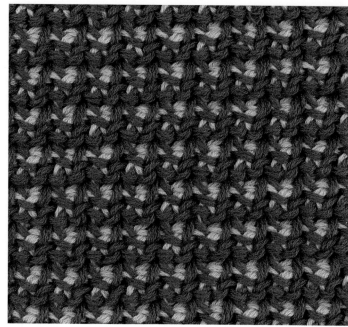

MATERIALS

- Medium (worsted) weight yarn:
  1 oz/50 yds/28g 2 colors A and B
- Size H/8/5mm double-ended hook used
  for photographed block

PATTERN NOTE

Read General Instructions on pages 5–7 before beginning pattern.

INSTRUCTIONS

STITCH PATTERN

Row 1: With color A, ch 24 or even number of chs, pull up lp in 2nd ch from hook, pull up lp in each ch across, turn. *(24 lps on hook)*

Row 2: With color B, work lps off hook, **do not turn**.

Row 3: Ch 1, sk first vertical bar, [yo, pull up lp in next 2 vertical bars at same time] across to last vertical bar, pull up lp in last vertical bar, turn.

Row 4: With color A, work lps off hook, **do not turn**.

Row 5: Rep row 3.

Rows 6–44: [Rep rows 2–5 consecutively] 10 times, ending last rep with row 4.

Row 45: Ch 1, sk first vertical bar, sl st in each vertical bar across. Fasten off. ■

number 44

design by Mary Ann Sipes

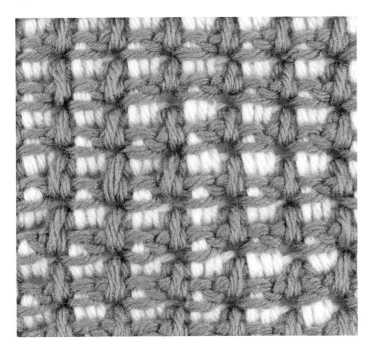

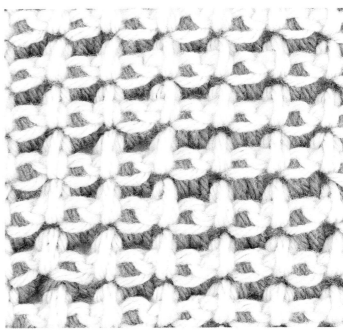

MATERIALS
- Medium (worsted) weight yarn:
  1 oz/50 yds/28g 2 colors A and B
- Size K/10½/6.5mm double-ended hook
  used for photographed block

4 MEDIUM

PATTERN NOTE
Read General Instructions on pages 5–7 before beginning pattern.

INSTRUCTIONS
STITCH PATTERN
Row 1: With color A, ch 16 or even number of chs, pull up lp in 2nd ch from hook, yo, pull up lp in same ch, [sk next ch, pull up lp in next ch, yo, pull up lp in same ch] across, turn. *(25 lps on hook)*

Row 2: With color B, pull through 1 lp on hook, [ch 1, yo, pull through 4 lps hook] across, **do not turn**.

Row 3: Ch 1, [pull up lp in next ch sp, yo, pull up lp in same sp] across, turn.

Row 4: With color A, pull through 1 lp on hook, [ch 1, yo, pull through 4 lps hook] across, **do not turn**.

Row 5: Ch 1, [pull up lp in next ch sp, yo, pull up lp in same sp] across, turn.

Rows 6–32: [Rep rows 2–5 consecutively] 7 times, ending last rep with row 4. At end of last row, fasten off. ■

number 45

design by Ann Parnell

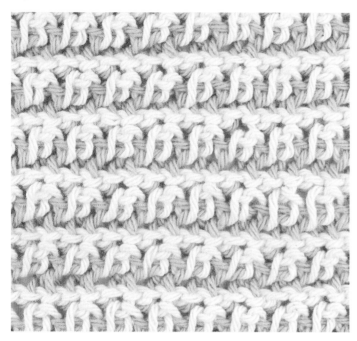

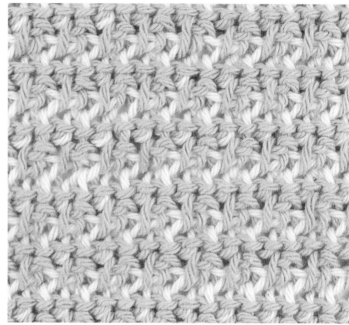

MATERIALS
■ Medium (worsted) weight yarn:
   1 oz/50 yds/28g 2 colors A and B
■ Size H/8/5mm double-ended hook used
   for photographed block

PATTERN NOTE
Read General Instructions on pages 5–7 before beginning pattern.

INSTRUCTIONS
STITCH PATTERN
Row 1: With color A, ch 32 or even number of chs, pull up lp in 2nd ch from hook, pull up lp in each ch across, turn. *(32 lps on hook)*

Row 2: With color B, work lps off hook, **do not turn**.

Row 3: Ch 1, sk first vertical bar, pull up lp in top strand of first **horizontal bar** *(see illustration)*, [yo, sk next horizontal bar, pull up lp in top strand of next horizontal bar] across, turn.

Horizontal Bar

Row 4: With color A, work lps off hook, **do not turn**.

Row 5: Rep row 3.

Rows 6–48: [Rep rows 2–5 consecutively] 11 times, ending last rep with row 4. At end of last row, fasten off. ■

number 46

design by Ann Parnell

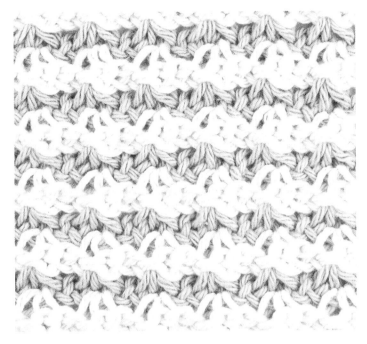

MATERIALS
- Medium (worsted) weight yarn:
  1 oz/50 yds/28g 2 colors A and B
- Size H/8/5mm double-ended hook used
  for photographed block

4 MEDIUM

PATTERN NOTE
Read General Instructions on pages 5–7 before beginning pattern.

INSTRUCTIONS
STITCH PATTERN
Row 1: With color A, ch 32 or in multiples of 3 plus 2 chs, pull up lp in 2nd ch from hook, pull up lp in each ch across, turn. *(32 lps on hook)*

Row 2: With color B, pull through 1 lp on hook, ch 1, yo, pull through 4 lps on hook *(completes a ch-2 and a shell)*, *ch 2, yo, pull through 4 lps on hook *(completes a ch-3 and a shell)* across to last 2 lps on hook, ch 1, yo, pull through last 2 lps on hook, **do not turn**.

Row 3: Ch 1, pull up lp in top strand of first **horizontal bar** *(see illustration)*, [sk next shell, pull up lp in next 3 chs] across to last ch-2, pull up lp in last 2 chs, pull up lp in last vertical bar, turn.

Horizontal Bar

Rows 4 & 5: With color A, rep rows 2 and 3.

Rows 6–28: [Rep rows 2–5 consecutively] 6 times, ending last rep with row 2. At end of last row, fasten off. ■

design by Ann Parnell

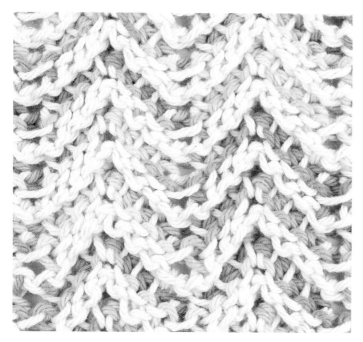

MATERIALS

- Medium (worsted) weight yarn:
  1 oz/50 yds/28g 2 colors A and B
- Size H/8/5mm double-ended hook used
  for photographed block

4 MEDIUM

PATTERN NOTE

Read General Instructions on pages 5–7 before beginning pattern.

INSTRUCTIONS

STITCH PATTERN

Row 1: With color A, ch 34 or in multiples of 9 plus 7 chs, pull up lp in 2nd ch from hook, pull up lp in next ch, (pull up lp, yo, pull up lp) in next ch, *pull up lp in each of next 3 chs, sk next 2 chs, pull up lp in each of next 3 chs, (pull up lp, yo, pull up lp) in next ch, rep from * across to last 3 chs, pull up lp in each of last 3 chs, turn. *(36 lps on hook)*

Row 2: With color B, work lps off hook, **do not turn**.

Row 3: Sk first 2 vertical bars, pull up lp in each of next 2 vertical bars, (pull up lp, yo, pull up lp) in next vertical bar, *pull up lp in each of next 3 vertical bars, sk next 2 vertical bars, pull up lp in each of next 3 vertical bars, (pull up lp, yo, pull up lp) in next vertical bar, rep from * across to last 4 vertical bars, pull up lp in each of next 2 vertical bars, sk next vertical bar, pull up lp in last vertical bar, turn.

Row 4: With color A, work lps off hook, **do not turn**.

Row 5: Rep row 3.

Rows 6–40: [Rep rows 2–5 consecutively] 9 times, ending last rep with row 4. At end of last row, fasten off. ■

design by Ann Parnell

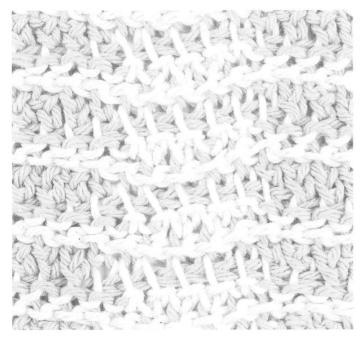

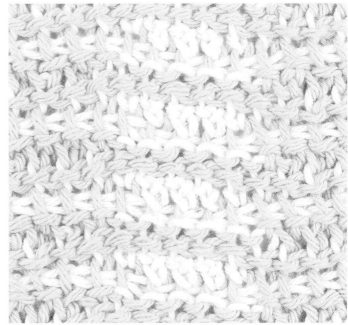

MATERIALS
- Medium (worsted) weight yarn:
  1 oz/50 yds/28g 2 colors A and B
- Size K/10½/6.5mm double-ended hook
  used for photographed block

4 MEDIUM

PATTERN NOTE
Read General Instructions on pages 5–7 before beginning pattern.

SPECIAL STITCHES
Single chain loop (single ch lp): Pull up lp in next vertical bar, yo, pull through 1 lp on hook.

Double chain loop (double ch lp): Pull up lp in next vertical bar, [yo, pull through 1 lp on hook] twice.

INSTRUCTIONS
STITCH PATTERN
Row 1: With color A, ch 25 or in multiples of 10 plus 5 chs, yo, pull up lp in 3rd ch from hook, [yo, sk next ch, pull up lp in next ch] across. *(25 lps on hook)*

Row 2: With color B, work lps off hook, **do not turn**.

Row 3: Sk first vertical bar, pull up lp in each of next 4 vertical bars, ***single ch lp** (see Special Stitches) in next vertical bar, **double ch lp** (see Special Stitches) in each of next 3 vertical bars, single ch lp in next vertical bar, pull up lp in each of next 5 vertical bars, rep from * across.

Row 4: With color A, work lps off hook, **do not turn**.

Row 5: Ch 1, sk first vertical bar, double ch lp in each of next 4 vertical bars, [pull up lp in each of next 5 vertical bars, single ch lp in next vertical bar, double ch lp in each of next 3 vertical bars, single ch lp in next vertical bar] across, turn.

Rows 6–36: Rep rows 2–5 consecutively] 8 times, ending last rep with row 4. At end of last row, fasten off. ∎

design by Ann Parnell

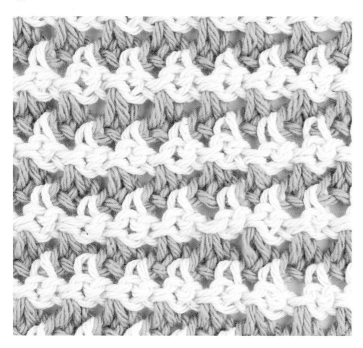

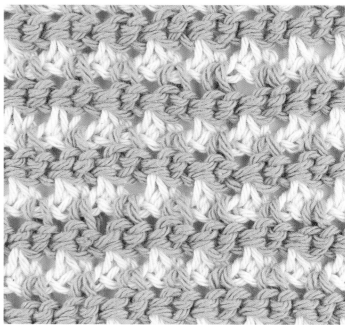

MATERIALS

- Medium (worsted) weight yarn:
  1 oz/50 yds/28g 2 colors A and B
- Size K/10½/6.5mm double-ended hook
  used for photographed block

PATTERN NOTE

Read General Instructions on pages 5–7 before beginning pattern.

INSTRUCTIONS

STITCH PATTERN

Row 1: With color A, ch 27 or an odd number of chs, pull up lp in 2nd ch from hook, pull up lp in each ch across, turn. *(27 lps on hook)*

Row 2: With color B, pull through 1 lp on hook, *ch 1, yo, pull through 2 lps on hook *(completes a ch-2 and a shell)*, rep from * across, **do not turn.**

Row 3: Working in top strands of chs only, ch 1, pull up lp in each ch across, turn. *(27 lps on hook)*

Rows 4 & 5: With color A, rep rows 2 and 3.

Rows 6–36: [Rep rows 2–5 consecutively] 8 times, ending last rep with row 4. At end of last row, fasten off. ■

number 50

MATERIALS
- Medium (worsted) weight yarn:
  1 oz/50 yds/28g 2 colors A and B
- Size K/10½/6.5mm double-ended hook
  used for photographed block

4 MEDIUM

PATTERN NOTE
Read General Instructions on pages 5–7 before beginning pattern.

INSTRUCTIONS
STITCH PATTERN
Row 1: With color A, ch 26 or in multiples of 3 plus 2 chs, pull up lp in 2nd ch from hook, pull up lp in each ch across, turn. *(26 lps on hook)*

Row 2: With color B, work lps off hook, *do not turn.*

Row 3: Ch 1, sk first vertical bar, pull up lp in each vertical bar across, turn.

Row 4: With color A, pull through 1 lp on hook, *ch 2, pull through 4 lps on hook *(completes a ch-3 and a shell)*, rep from * across to last 2 lps on hook, **do not turn**.

Row 5: Ch 1, pull up lp in top strand of next **horizontal bar** *(see illustration)*, working in top strands of chs and sk all shells, pull up lp in each ch across, turn. *(26 lps on hook)*

Horizontal Bar

Rows 6–42: [Rep rows 2–5 consecutively] 10 times, ending last rep with row 2. At end of last row, fasten off. ∎

number 51

design by Tammy Hildebrand

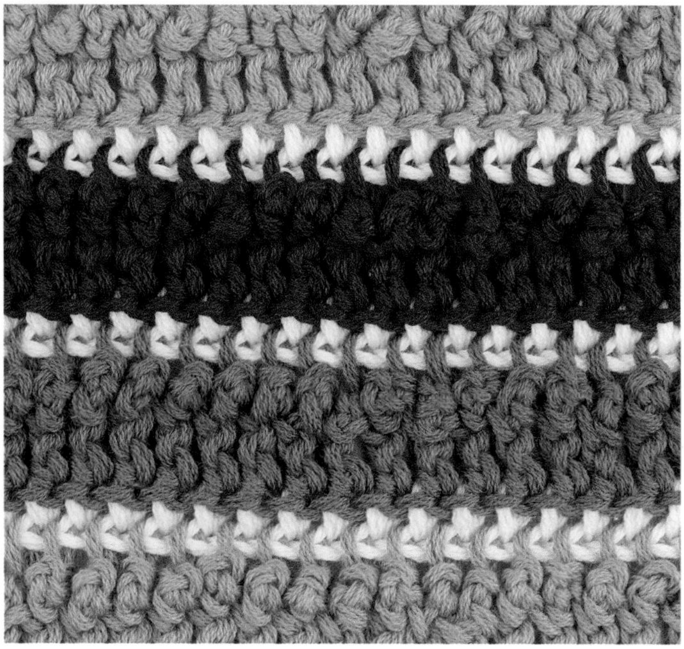

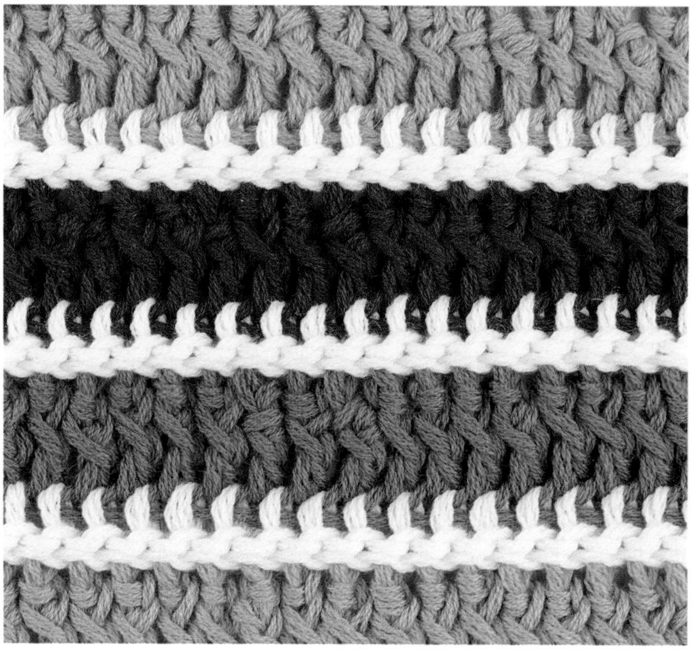

MATERIALS

- Medium (worsted) weight yarn:
  1 oz/50 yds/28g 2 colors A and B
- Size K/10½/6.5mm double-ended hook used for photographed block

PATTERN NOTE

Read General Instructions on pages 5–7 before beginning pattern.

SPECIAL STITCH

Double crochet loop (dc lp): Yo, insert hook in place indicated, yo, pull lp through, yo, pull through 2 lps on hook.

INSTRUCTIONS

STITCH PATTERN

Row 1: With color A, ch 30 or even number of chs, pull up lp in 2nd ch from hook, pull up lp in each ch across, turn. *(30 lps on hook)*

Row 2: With color B, work lps off hook, **do not turn.**

Row 3: Ch 2, ***dc lp** *(see Special Stitch)* in top strand of next **horizontal bar** *(see illustration)*, ch 3, sl st in 3rd ch from hook, rep across to last horizontal bar, dc lp in top strand of last horizontal bar, turn.

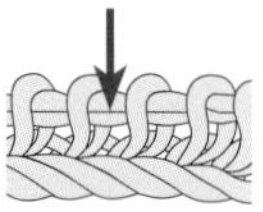

Horizontal Bar

Row 4: With color A, work lps off hook, **do not turn.**

Row 5: Ch 1, pull up lp in top strand of each horizontal bar across, turn.

Rows 6–32: [Rep rows 2–5 consecutively] 7 times, ending last rep with row 4.

Row 33: Ch 1, sk first vertical bar, sl st in each vertical bar across. Fasten off. ■

number 52

design by Tammy Hildebrand

MATERIALS
- Medium (worsted) weight yarn:
  1 oz/50 yds/28g 2 colors A and B
- Size G/6/4mm double-ended hook
  used for photographed block

4
MEDIUM

PATTERN NOTE
Read General Instructions on pages 5–7 before beginning pattern.

SPECIAL STITCH
Double crochet loop (dc lp): Yo, insert hook in place indicated, yo, pull lp through, yo, pull through 2 lps on hook.

INSTRUCTIONS
STITCH PATTERN
Row 1: With color A, ch 35 or in multiples of 4 plus 3 chs, **dc lp** *(see Special Stitch)* in 3rd ch from hook, dc lp in each ch across, turn. *(34 lps on hook)*

Row 2: With color B, work lps off hook, **do not turn**.

Row 3: Ch 1, sk first vertical bar, dc lp in each vertical bar across, turn.

Row 4: With color A, pull through 1 lp on hook, *ch 3, yo, pull through 5 lps on hook *(completes a ch-4 and a shell)*, rep from * across to last 2 lps on hook, yo, pull through last 2 lps on hook, **do not turn**.

Row 5: Ch 2, sk all shells, dc lp in each ch across, dc lp in last vertical bar, turn. *(34 lps on hook)*

Rows 6–28: [Rep rows 2–5 consecutively] 6 times, ending last rep with row 4.

Row 29: Ch 2, sk first vertical bar, hdc in each vertical bar across. Fasten off. ∎

design by Eleanor Miles-Bradley

MATERIALS
- Medium (worsted) weight yarn:
  1 oz/50 yds/28g 2 colors A & B
- Size H/8/5mm double-ended hook
  used for photographed block

4 MEDIUM

PATTERN NOTE
Read General Instructions on pages 5–7 before beginning pattern.

SPECIAL STITCHES
Double crochet loop (dc lp): Yo, insert hook in next ch or vertical bar, yo, pull lp through, yo, pull through 2 lps on hook.

Cluster (cl): 3 dc lps in next ch or vertical bar, yo, pull through 3 lps on hook.

INSTRUCTIONS
STITCH PATTERN
Row 1: With A, ch 32 or in multiples of 17 plus 15 chs, **cl** *(see Special Stitches)* in 2nd ch from hook, pull up lp in next ch, [cl in next ch, pull up lp in next ch] twice, 3 **dc lps** *(see Special Stitches)* in next ch, pull up lp in next ch, [cl in next ch, pull up lp in next ch] 3 times, *sk next 2 chs, pull up lp in next ch, [cl in next ch, pull up lp in next ch] 3 times, 3 dc lps in next ch, pull up lp in next ch, [cl in next ch, pull up lp in next ch] 3 times, rep from * across, turn.

Row 2: With B, pull through 1 lp on hook, *[yo, pull through 2 lps on hook] 15 times, yo, pull through 3 lps on hook, rep from * across, ending with [yo, pull through 2 lps on hook] across, **do not turn**.

Row 3: Sk first 2 vertical bars, [cl in next vertical bar, pull up lp in next vertical bar] 3 times, 3 dc lps in next vertical bar, pull up lp in next vertical bar, [cl in next vertical bar, pull up lp in next vertical bar] 3 times, *sk next 2 vertical bars, pull up lp in next vertical bar, [cl in next vertical bar, pull up lp in next vertical bar] 3 times, 3 dc lps in next vertical bar, pull up lp in next vertical bar, [cl in next vertical bar, pull up lp in next vertical bar] 3 times, rep from * across, ending with [cl in next vertical bar, pull up lp in next vertical bar] twice, cl in next vertical bar, pull up lp in last 2 vertical bars at same time, turn.

Next rows: Alternating colors, rep rows 2 and 3 alternately, ending with row 2. At end of last row, fasten off. ■

number 54

design by Tammy Hildebrand

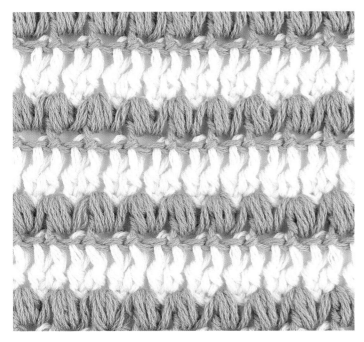
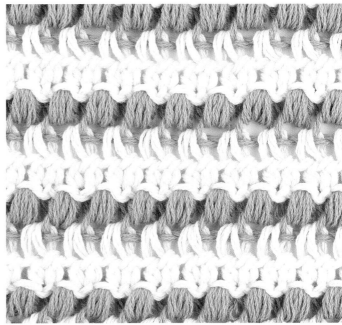

MATERIALS
- Medium (worsted) weight yarn:
  1 oz/50 yds/28g 2 colors A and B
- Size K/10½/6.5mm double-ended hook
  used for photographed block

4 MEDIUM

PATTERN NOTE
Read General Instructions on pages 5–7 before beginning pattern.

SPECIAL STITCH
Double crochet loop (dc lp): Yo, insert hook in place indicated, yo, pull lp through, yo, pull through 2 lps on hook.

INSTRUCTIONS
STITCH PATTERN
Row 1: With color A, ch 34 or even number of chs, **dc lp** (see Special Stitch) in 3rd ch from hook, dc lp in each ch across, turn. (33 lps on hook)

Row 2: With color B, work lps off hook, **do not turn**.

Row 3: Ch 1, *sk next **horizontal bar** (see illustration), (yo, pull up lp) 3 times in top strand of next horizontal bar, rep across to last 2 horizontal bars, sk next horizontal bar, pull up lp in top strand of last horizontal bar, turn.

Horizontal Bar

Row 4: With color A, pull through 1 lp on hook, *ch 1, yo, pull through 7 lps on hook (completes a ch-2 and a puff st), rep from * across to last 2 lps on hook, ch 1, pull through last 2 lps on hook (completes a ch-2 and a vertical bar), **do not turn**.

Row 5: Ch 1, sk all puff sts, dc lp in each ch across, turn. (33 lps on hook)

Rows 6–32: [Rep rows 2–5 consecutively] 7 times, ending last rep with row 4.

Row 33: Ch 1, sk all puff sts, hdc in each ch across. Fasten off. ■

design by Tammy Hildebrand

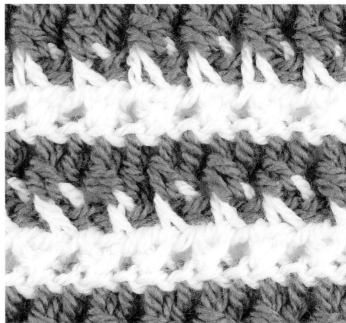

MATERIALS
- Medium (worsted) weight yarn:
  1 oz/50 yds/28g 2 colors A and B
- Size K/10½/6.5mm double-ended hook
  used for photographed block

4
MEDIUM

PATTERN NOTE
Read General Instructions on pages 5–7 before beginning pattern.

SPECIAL STITCHES
Double crochet loop (dc lp): Yo, insert hook in place indicated, yo, pull lp through, yo, pull through 2 lps on hook.

Cross-stitch (cross-st): Sk next ch, st or **horizontal bar** (see illustration), dc lp in next ch, st or top strand of next horizontal bar, working in front of last dc lp worked, dc lp in sk ch, st or top strand of horizontal bar.

Horizontal Bar

INSTRUCTIONS

STITCH PATTERN
Row 1: With color A, ch 32 or even number of chs, **dc lp** (see Special Stitches) in 3rd ch from hook, **cross-st** (see Special Stitches) across to last ch, dc lp in last ch, turn. (31 lps on hook)

Row 2: With color B, work lps off hook, **do not turn.**

Row 3: Ch 1, sk first vertical bar, dc lp in next vertical bar, working in vertical bars, cross-st across to last vertical bar, dc lp in last vertical bar, turn.

Row 4: With color A, work lps off hook, **do not turn.**

Row 5: Ch 1, dc lp in top strand of first horizontal bar, working in horizontal bars, cross-st across to last horizontal bar, dc lp in top strand of last horizontal bar, turn.

Rows 6–20: [Rep rows 2–5 consecutively] 4 times, ending last rep with row 4.

Row 21: Ch 1, hdc in top strand of each horizontal bar across. Fasten off. ■

design by Tammy Hildebrand

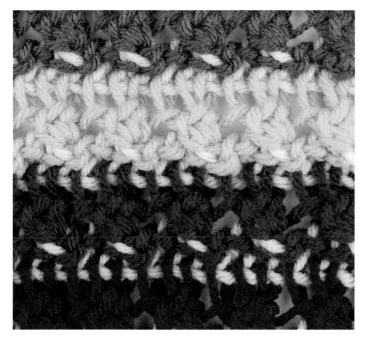

MATERIALS
- Medium (worsted) weight yarn:
  1 oz/50 yds/28g of colors A and several
  of different colors B
- Size K/10½/6.5mm double-ended hook
  used for photographed block

4 MEDIUM

PATTERN NOTE
Read General Instructions on pages 5–7 before beginning pattern.

SPECIAL STITCH
Double crochet loop (dc lp): Yo, insert hook in place indicated, yo, pull lp through, yo, pull through 2 lps on hook.

INSTRUCTIONS
STITCH PATTERN
Row 1: With color A, ch 29 or in multiples of 3 plus 2 chs, pull up lp in 2nd ch from hook, pull up lp in each ch across, turn. *(29 lps on hook)*

Row 2: With color B, work lps off hook, **do not turn.**

Row 3: Ch 2, sk first 2 vertical bars, **dc lp** *(see Special Stitch)* in each of next 2 vertical bars, working in front of last 2 dc lps worked, dc lp in 2nd sk vertical bar, [sk next vertical bar, dc lp in each of next 2 vertical bars, working in front of last 2 dc lps worked, dc lp in sk vertical bar] across to last vertical bar, dc lp in last vertical bar, turn.

Row 4: With color A, work lps off hook, **do not turn.**

Row 5: Ch 1, pull up lp in top strand of each **horizontal bar** *(see illustration)* across, turn.

Horizontal Bar

Rows 6–36: [Rep rows 2–5 consecutively] 8 times, ending last rep with row 4.

Row 37: Ch 1, sl st in top strand of each horizontal bar across. Fasten off. ■

design by Tammy Hildebrand

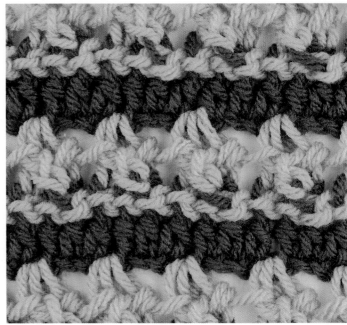

MATERIALS
- Medium (worsted) weight yarn:
  1 oz/50 yds/28g 2 colors A and B
- Size K/10½/6.5mm double-ended hook
  used for photographed block

4 MEDIUM

PATTERN NOTE
Read General Instructions on pages 5–7 before beginning pattern.

SPECIAL STITCH
Double crochet loop (dc lp): Yo, insert hook in place indicated, yo, pull lp through, yo, pull through 2 lps on hook.

INSTRUCTIONS
STITCH PATTERN
Row 1: With color A, ch 27 or in multiples of 3 chs, **dc lp** (see Special Stitch) in 3rd ch from hook, dc lp in each ch across, turn. (26 lps on hook)

Row 2: With color B, work lps off hook, **do not turn.**

Row 3: Ch 3, sk first vertical bar, [sk next 2 vertical bars, dc lp in next vertical bar, working in front of last dc lp made, dc lp in 2nd sk vertical bar, dc lp in first sk vertical bar] across to last vertical bar, dc lp in last vertical bar.

Row 4: With color A, pull through 1 lp on hook, yo, pull through 4 lps on hook, *ch 2, yo, pull through 4 lps on hook (completes ch-3 and shell), rep from * across to last 2 lps on hook, ch 2, pull through last 2 lps on hook (completes ch-3 and vertical bar), turn.

Row 5: Ch 1, sk all shells, dc lp in each ch across to last **horizontal bar** (see illustration), dc lp in top strand of last horizontal bar, **do not turn.**

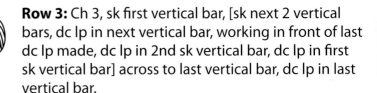

Horizontal Bar

Rows 6–20: [Rep rows 2–5 consecutively] 4 times, ending last rep with row 4.

Row 21: Ch 2, sk all shells, hdc in each ch across with hdc in top strand of last horizontal bar. Fasten off. ∎

design by Tammy Hildebrand

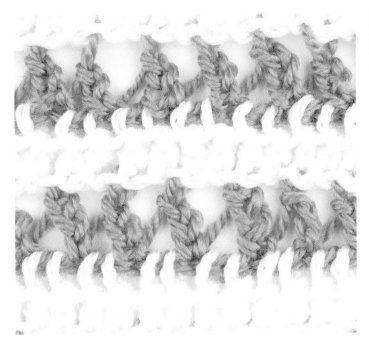

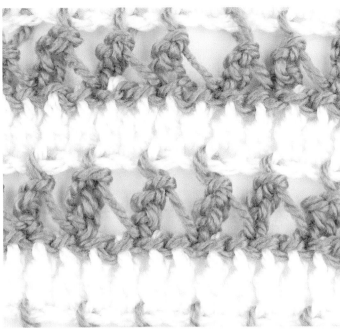

MATERIALS
- Medium (worsted) weight yarn:
  1 oz/50 yds/28g 2 colors A and B
- Size K/10½/6.5mm double-ended hook
  used for photographed block

4 MEDIUM

PATTERN NOTE
Read General Instructions on pages 5–7 before beginning pattern.

SPECIAL STITCHES
Single crochet loop (sc lp): Pull up lp in place indicated, yo, pull lp through, ch 1.

Double crochet loop (dc lp): Yo, insert hook in place indicated, yo, pull lp through, yo, pull through 2 lps on hook.

INSTRUCTIONS
STITCH PATTERN
Row 1: With color A, ch 26 or even number of chs, **dc lp** (see Special Stitches) in 2nd ch from hook, dc lp in each ch across, turn. (26 lps on hook)

Row 2: With color B, work lps off hook, **do not turn**.

Row 3: Ch 2, **sc lp** (see Special Stitches) in top strand of first **horizontal bar** (see illustration), ch 2, [sk next horizontal bar, sc lp in top strand of next horizontal bar, ch 2] across, turn.

Horizontal Bar

Row 4: With color A, pull through 1 lp on hook, yo, pull through next 2 lps on hook, *ch 1, yo, pull through 2 lps on hook (completes ch-2 and vertical bar), rep from * across, **do not turn**.

Row 5: Ch 2, dc lp in each ch across to last horizontal bar, dc lp in top strand of last horizontal bar, turn.

Rows 6–16: [Rep rows 2–5 consecutively] 3 times, ending last rep with row 4.

Row 17: Ch 2, hdc in top strand of each ch or horizontal bar across. Fasten off. ■

design by Darla Fanton

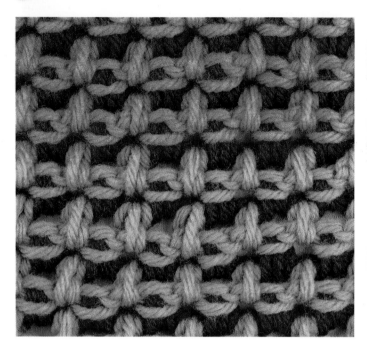

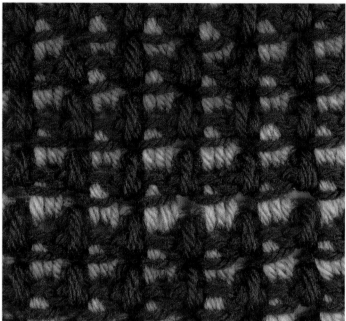

MATERIALS
- Medium (worsted) weight yarn:
  1 oz/50 yds/28g each 2 colors A and B
- Size K/10½/6.5mm double-ended hook
  used for photographed block

PATTERN NOTE
Read General Instructions on pages 5–7 before beginning pattern.

INSTRUCTIONS
STITCH PATTERN
Row 1: With color A, ch 22 or even number of chs, pull up lp in 2nd ch from hook, yo, pull up lp in same ch, [sk next ch, pull up lp in next ch, yo, pull up lp in same ch] across, turn. *(34 lps on hook)*

Row 2: With color B, pull through 1 lp on hook, [ch 1, yo, pull through 4 lps on hook] across, **do not turn**.

Row 3: Ch 1, pull up lp in first ch sp, yo, pull up lp in same sp, [pull up lp in next ch sp, yo, pull up lp in same sp] across, turn.

Rows 4 & 5: With color A, rep rows 2 and 3.

Rows 6–44: [Rep rows 2–5 consecutively] 10 times, ending last rep with row 4.

Row 45: Ch 1, sl st twice in each ch sp across. Fasten off. ■

design by Darla Fanton

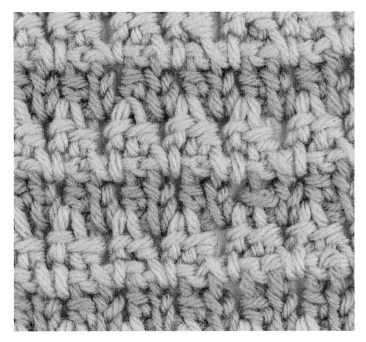

MATERIALS

- Medium (worsted) weight yarn:
  1 oz/50 yds/28g each 2 colors A and B
- Size K/10½/6.5mm double-ended hook
  used for photographed block

4
MEDIUM

PATTERN NOTE

Read General Instructions on pages 5–7 before beginning pattern.

INSTRUCTIONS

STITCH PATTERN

Row 1: With color A, ch 23 or odd number of chs, pull up lp in 2nd ch from hook, pull up lp in each ch across, turn. *(23 lps on hook)*

Row 2: With color B, work lps off hook, **do not turn**.

Row 3: Sk first **horizontal bar** *(see illustration)*, *pull up lp in sp under next horizontal bar, ch 2, yo, insert hook in next vertical bar, yo, pull lp through bar and through 1 lp on hook**, sk next vertical bar, rep from * across, ending last rep at **, turn.

Horizontal Bar

Rows 4 & 5: With color A, rep rows 2 and 3.

Rows 6–24: [Rep rows 2–5 consecutively] 5 times, ending last rep with row 4.

Row 25: Ch 1, sl st in top strand of each horizontal bar across. Fasten off. ■

number 61

design by Dorris Brooks

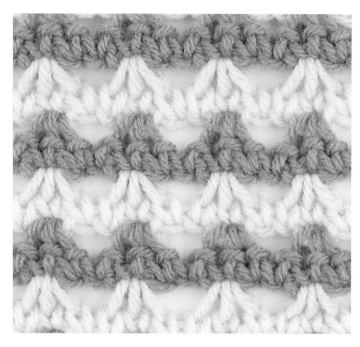 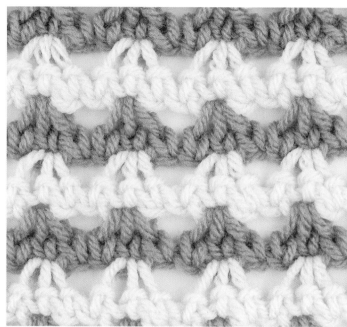

MATERIALS
- Medium (worsted) weight yarn:
  1 oz/50 yds/28g 2 colors A and B
- K/10½/6.5mm double-ended hook used for photographed block

PATTERN NOTE
Read General Instructions on pages 5–7 before beginning pattern.

SPECIAL STITCHES
Single crochet loop (sc lp): Insert hook in place indicated, yo, pull up lp, ch 1.

Shell: Yo, pull through 4 lps on hook.

INSTRUCTIONS
STITCH PATTERN
Row 1: With color A, ch 20 or in multiples of 3 plus 2 chs, **sc lp** *(see Special Stitches)* in 2nd ch from hook, sc lp in each ch across, turn. *(20 lps on hook)*

Row 2: With color B, pull through 1 lp on hook, ch 2, **shell** *(see Special Stitches)*, [ch 3, shell] across to last 2 lps on hook, ch 2, yo, pull through last 2 lps on hook, **do not turn**.

Row 3: Ch 1, sk first vertical bar, sc lp in next ch, [sk next ch, sc lp in next shell, sc lp in next 2 chs] across, turn.

Rows 4 & 5: With color A, rep rows 2 and 3.

Rows 6–21: [Rep rows 2–5 consecutively] 4 times. At end of last row, **do not turn**.

Row 22: Rep row 4.

Row 23: Ch 1, sk first vertical bar, sl st in next ch, [sk next ch, sl st in next shell, sl st in next 2 chs] across to last vertical bar, sl st in last vertical bar. Fasten off. ■

design by Dorris Brooks

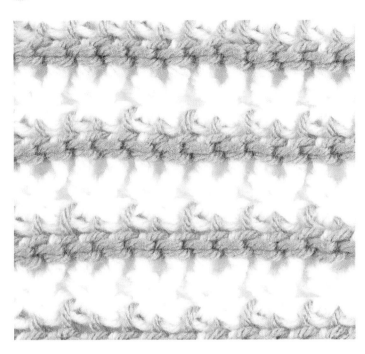

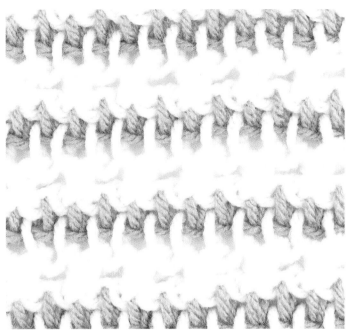

MATERIALS

- Medium (worsted) weight yarn:
  1 oz/50 yds/28g 2 colors A and B
- K/10½/6.5mm double-ended hook used
  for photographed block

4 MEDIUM

PATTERN NOTE

Read General Instructions on pages 5–7 before beginning pattern.

SPECIAL STITCH

Cross-stitch (cross-st): Sk next **horizontal bar** (see illustration), yo, pull up lp in top strand of next horizontal bar, yo, pull through 2 lps on hook, working around st just worked, yo, pull up lp in top strand of sk horizontal bar, [yo, pull through 2 lps on hook] twice.

Horizontal Bar

INSTRUCTIONS

STITCH PATTERN

Row 1: With color A, ch 18 or in multiples of 2 chs, pull up lp in 2nd ch from hook, pull up lp in each ch across, turn. *(18 lps on hook)*

Row 2: With color B, work lps off hook, **do not turn**.

Row 3: Ch 1, sk first vertical bar, **cross-st** *(see Special Stitch)* across to last horizontal bar, pull up lp in last horizontal bar, turn.

Rows 4 & 5: With color A, rep rows 2 and 3.

Rows 6–20: [Rep rows 2–5 consecutively] 4 times, ending last rep with row 4.

Row 21: Ch 1, sk first vertical bar, sl st in top strand of each horizontal bar across. Fasten off. ∎

design by Dorris Brooks

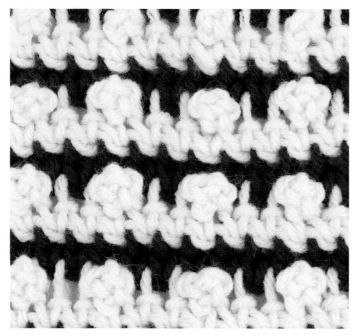

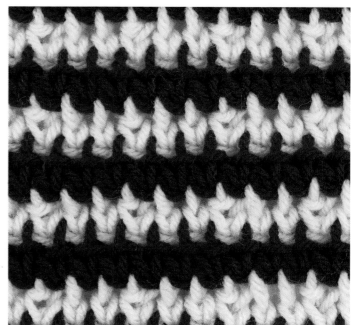

MATERIALS
- Medium (worsted) weight yarn:
  1 oz/50 yds/28g 2 colors A and B
- K/10½/6.5mm double-ended hook used
  for photographed block

4 MEDIUM

PATTERN NOTE
Read General Instructions on pages 5–7 before beginning pattern.

SPECIAL STITCHES
Single crochet loop (sc lp): Pull up lp in place indicated, ch 1.

Picot: Ch 2, sl st in 2nd ch from hook.

INSTRUCTIONS
STITCH PATTERN
Row 1: With color A, ch 20 or in multiples of 3 plus 2 chs, **sc lp** *(see Special Stitches)* in 2nd ch from hook, sc lp in each ch across, turn. *(20 lps on hook)*

Row 2: With color B, work lps off hook, **do not turn**.

Row 3: Ch 1, sk first vertical bar, sc lp in top strand of next **horizontal bar** *(see illustration)*, *pull up lp in top strand of next horizontal bar, **picot** *(see Special Stitches)*, sc lp in top strand of each of next 2 horizontal bars, rep from * across, turn.

Horizontal Bar

Rows 4 & 5: With color A, rep rows 2 and 3, **do not turn**.

Rows 6–24: [Rep rows 2–5 consecutively] 5 times, ending last rep with row 4.

Row 25: Ch 1, sk first vertical bar, sc in top strand of each horizontal bar across. Fasten off. ■

design by Dorris Brooks

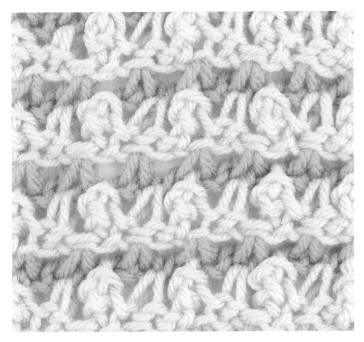

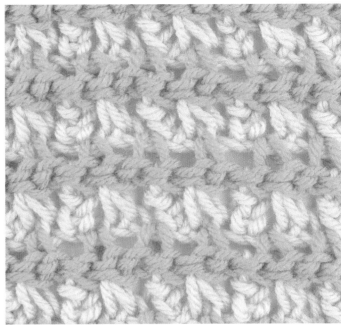

MATERIALS
- Medium (worsted) weight yarn:
  1 oz/50 yds/28g 2 colors A and B
- K/10½/6.5mm double-ended hook used
  for photographed block

4 MEDIUM

PATTERN NOTE
Read General Instructions on pages 5–7 before beginning pattern.

INSTRUCTIONS
STITCH PATTERN
Row 1: With color A, ch 21 or in multiples of 3 chs, pull up lp in 2nd ch from hook, pull up lp in each ch across, turn. *(21 lps on hook)*

Row 2: With color B, work lps off hook, **do not turn.**

Row 3: Ch 1, sk first vertical bar, pull up lp in top strand of next **horizontal bar** *(see illustration)*, ch 3, [pull up lp in top strand of next 3 horizontal bars, ch 3] across to last horizontal bar, pull up lp in top strand of last horizontal bar, turn.

Horizontal Bar

Row 4: With color A, pull through 1 lp on hook, *yo, pull through 2 lps on hook, ch 1, yo, pull through 3 lps on hook *(completes ch-2 and shell)* across to last 3 lps on hook, [yo, pull through 2 lps on hook] twice, **do not turn.**

Row 5: Ch 1, sk first vertical bar, pull up lp in top strand of each horizontal bar or ch across, turn.

Row 6: With color B, pull through 1 lp on hook, *ch 1, yo, pull through 3 lps on hook *(completes ch-2 and a shell)*, rep from * across to last 2 lps on hook, yo, pull through last 2 lps on hook, **do not turn.**

Row 7: Ch 1, sk first vertical bar, pull up lp in top strand of next horizontal bar, ch 3, [sk all shells, pull up lp in top strand in each of next 3 chs, ch 3] across to last ch, pull up lp in top strand of last ch, turn.

Rows 8–24: [Rep rows 4–7 consecutively] 5 times, ending last rep with row 4.

Row 25: Ch 1, sk first vertical bar, sc in top strand of each horizontal bar or ch across. Fasten off. ■

design by Dorris Brooks

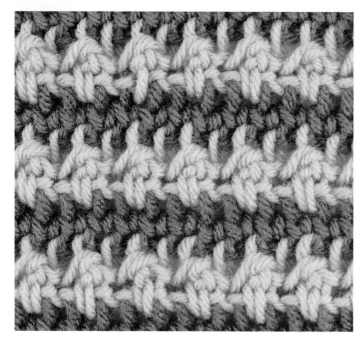

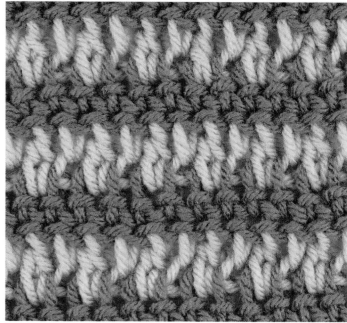

MATERIALS
- Medium (worsted) weight yarn:
  1 oz/50 yds/28g 2 colors A and B
- Size K/10½/6.5mm double-ended hook
  used for photographed block

4 MEDIUM

PATTERN NOTE
Read General Instructions on pages 5–7 before beginning pattern.

SPECIAL STITCHES
Single crochet loop (sc lp): Pull up lp in place indicated, ch 1.

Knot stitch (knot st): Yo, pull up lp in indicated place, yo, pull through 1 lp on hook, yo, pull through 2 lps on hook.

INSTRUCTIONS
STITCH PATTERN
Row 1: With color A, ch 21 or odd number of chs, **sc lp** *(see Special Stitches)* in 2nd ch from hook, sc lp in each ch across, turn. *(21 lps on hook)*

Row 2: With color B, work lps off hook, **do not turn**.

Row 3: Ch 1, sk first vertical bar, **knot st** *(see Special Stitches)* in sp under next **horizontal bar** *(see illustration)*, [pull up lp in top strand of next horizontal bar, knot st in sp under next horizontal bar] across to last horizontal bar, sc lp in top strand of last horizontal bar, turn.

Horizontal Bar

Row 4: With color A, work lps off hook, **do not turn**.

Row 5: Ch 1, sk first vertical bar, sc lp in top strand of each horizontal bar across, turn.

Rows 6–20: [Rep rows 2–5 consecutively] 4 times, ending last rep with row 4.

Row 21: Ch 1, sk first vertical bar, sc in top strand of each horizontal bar across. Fasten off. ∎

number 66

design by Dorris Brooks

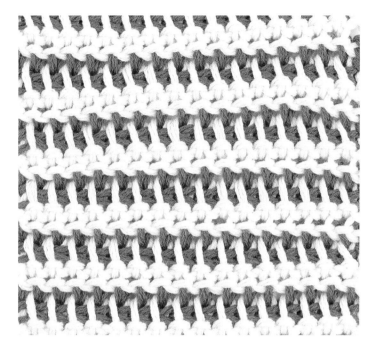

MATERIALS
- Medium (worsted) weight yarn: 1 oz/50 yds/28g 2 colors A and B
- Size H/8/5mm double-ended hook used for photographed block

4 MEDIUM

PATTERN NOTE
Read General Instructions on pages 5–7 before beginning pattern.

SPECIAL STITCH
Single crochet loop (sc lp): Pull up lp in place indicated, ch 1.

INSTRUCTIONS
STITCH PATTERN
Row 1: With color A, ch 18 or even number of chs, **sc lp** *(see Special Stitch)* in 2nd ch from hook, sc lp in each ch across, turn. *(18 lps on hook)*

Row 2: With color B, pull through 1 lp on hook, [yo, pull through 2 lps on hook] across, **do not turn**.

Row 3: Ch 1, sk first vertical bar, pull up lp in each vertical bar across, turn.

Row 4: With color A, work lps off hook, **do not turn**.

Row 5: Ch 1, sk first vertical bar, sc lp in top strand of each **horizontal bar** *(see illustration)* across, turn.

Horizontal Bar

Rows 6–28: [Rep rows 2–5 consecutively] 6 times, ending last rep with row 4.

Row 29: Ch 1, sk first vertical bar, sc in top strand of each horizontal bar across. Fasten off. ■

design by Dorris Brooks

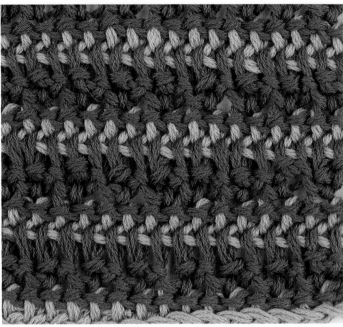

MATERIALS

- Medium (worsted) weight yarn:
  1 oz/50 yds/28g 2 colors A and B
- Size H/8/5mm double-ended hook used
  for photographed block

4 MEDIUM

PATTERN NOTE

Read General Instructions on pages 5–7 before beginning pattern.

INSTRUCTIONS

STITCH PATTERN

Row 1: With color A, ch 19 or odd number of chs, pull up lp in 2nd ch from hook, pull up lp in each ch across, turn. *(19 lps on hook)*

Row 2: With color B, work lps off hook, **do not turn**.

Row 3: [Ch 2, pull up lp in 2nd ch from hook, ch 1, sk next **horizontal bar** *(see illustration)*, pull up lp in top strand of next horizontal bar across, turn.

Horizontal Bar

Row 4: With color A, work lps off hook, **do not turn**.

Row 5: Ch 1, sk first vertical bar, pull up lp in top strand of each horizontal bar across, turn.

Rows 6–16: [Rep rows 2–5 consecutively] 3 times, ending last rep with row 4. At end of last row, fasten off B.

Row 17: With A, ch 1, sk first vertical bar, sl st in top strand of each horizontal bar across. Fasten off. ■

number 68

design by Dorris Brooks

MATERIALS
- Medium (worsted) weight yarn:
  1 oz/50 yds/28g 2 colors A and B
- Size K/10½/6.5mm double-ended hook
  used for photographed block

4 MEDIUM

PATTERN NOTE
Read General Instructions on pages 5–7 before beginning pattern.

SPECIAL STITCH
Single crochet loop (sc lp): Pull up lp in place indicated, ch 1.

INSTRUCTIONS
STITCH PATTERN
Row 1: With color A, ch 20 or in multiples of 5 chs, **sc lp** (see Special Stitch) in 2nd ch from hook, sc lp in each ch across, turn. (20 lps on hook)

Row 2: With color B, pull through 1 lp on hook, yo, pull through 2 lps on hook, ch 7, *[yo, pull through 2 lps on hook] 5 times, ch 7, rep from * across to last 4 lps on hook, [yo, pull through 2 lps on hook] 3 times, **do not turn**.

Row 3: Ch 1, sk first vertical bar, pull up lp in each vertical bar across, turn.

Row 4: With A, pull through 1 lp on hook, [yo, pull through 2 lps on hook] across, **do not turn**.

Row 5: Ch 1, sk first vertical bar, sc lp in top strand of next **horizontal bar** (see illustration), pull up lp in center ch of next ch lp on 2 rows before last, sk next horizontal bar on last row, [sc lp in top strand of next 4 horizontal bars, pull up lp in center ch of next ch lp on 2 rows before last, sk next horizontal bar on last row] across to last 2 vertical bars, sc lp in top strand of last 2 horizontal bars, turn.

Horizontal Bar

Rows 6–24: [Rep rows 2–5 consecutively] 5 times, ending last rep with row 4.

Row 25: Ch 1, sk first vertical bar, sc in top strand of each horizontal bar across. Fasten off. ■

design by Dorris Brooks

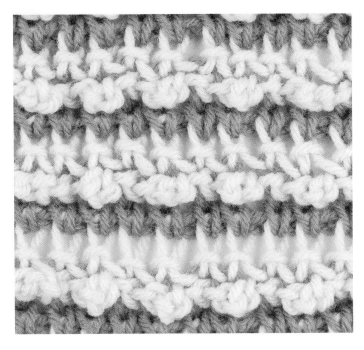

MATERIALS

- Medium (worsted) weight yarn:
  1 oz/50 yds/28g 2 colors A and B
- Size K/10½/6.5mm double-ended hook
  used for photographed block

PATTERN NOTE

Read General Instructions on pages 5–7 before beginning pattern.

SPECIAL STITCH

Single crochet loop (sc lp): Pull up lp in place indicated, ch 1.

INSTRUCTIONS

STITCH PATTERN

Row 1: With color A, ch 18 or even number of chs, **sc lp** *(see Special Stitch)* in 2nd ch from hook, sc lp in each ch across, turn. *(18 lps on hook)*

Row 2: With color B, pull through 1 lp on hook, ch 3, *[yo, pull through 2 lps on hook] twice, ch 3, rep

from * across to last 2 lps on hook, yo, pull through last 2 lps, **do not turn**.

Row 3: Ch 1, sk first vertical bar, sk all ch-3 sps, sc lp in each vertical bar across, turn.

Row 4: With color A, pull through 1 lp on hook, [yo, pull through 2 lps on hook] across, **do not turn**.

Row 5: Ch 1, sk first vertical bar; working over last row, sc lp in sp between front and back lps of each vertical bar across row before last, turn.

Rows 6–20: [Rep rows 2–5 consecutively] 4 times, ending last rep with row 4.

Row 21: Ch 1, sk first vertical bar; working over last row, sc in sp between front and back lps of each vertical bar across row before last. Fasten off. ■

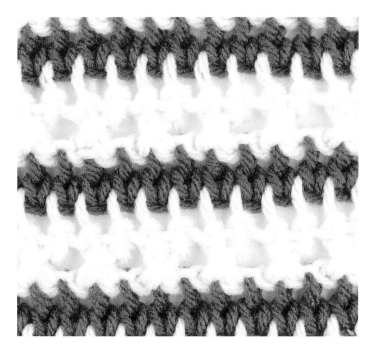

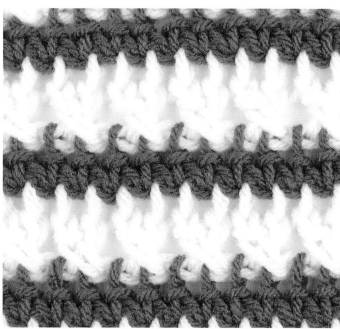

MATERIALS
- Medium (worsted) weight yarn:
  1 oz/50 yds/28g 2 colors A and B
- Size K/10½/6.5mm double-ended hook
  used for photographed block

4 MEDIUM

PATTERN NOTES
Read General Instructions on pages 5–7 before beginning pattern.

Chain-3 at beginning of row or round counts as first long double crochet loop, unless otherwise stated.

SPECIAL STITCHES
Single crochet loop (sc lp): Pull up lp in place indicated, ch 1.

Long double crochet loop (lng dc lp): Yo, pull up lp in indicated place, yo, pull through 2 lps on hook, ch 1.

Cross-stitch (cross-st): Sk next **horizontal bar** (see illustration), lng dc lp on top strand of next horizontal bar, working around st just worked, lng dc lp in top strand of horizontal bar just sk.

Horizontal Bar

INSTRUCTIONS
STITCH PATTERN
Row 1: With color A, ch 18 or even number of chs, **sc lp** (see Special Stitches) in 2nd ch from hook, sc lp in each ch across, turn. (18 lps on hook)

Row 2: With color B, work lps off hook, **do not turn.**

Row 3: Ch 3 (see Pattern Notes), **cross-st** (see Special Stitches) across to last horizontal bar, lng dc lp in top strand of last horizontal bar, turn.

Row 4: With color A, work lps off hook, **do not turn.**

Row 5: Ch 1, sk first vertical bar, sc lp in top strand of each horizontal bar across, turn.

Rows 6–16: [Rep rows 2–5 consecutively] 3 times, ending last rep with row 4.

Row 17: Ch 1, sk first vertical bar, sc in top strand of each horizontal bar across. Fasten off. ■

design by Dorris Brooks

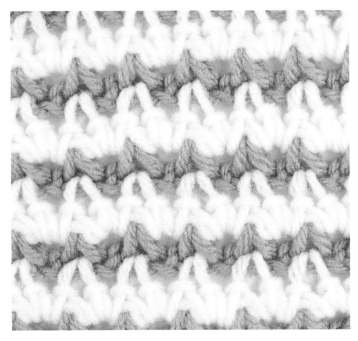

MATERIALS

- Medium (worsted) weight yarn:
  1 oz/50 yds/28g 2 colors A and B
- Size K/10½/6.5mm double-ended hook
  used for photographed block

4 MEDIUM

PATTERN NOTE

Read General Instructions on pages 5–7 before beginning pattern.

SPECIAL STITCH

Single crochet loop (sc lp): Pull up lp in place indicated, ch 1.

INSTRUCTIONS
STITCH PATTERN

Row 1: With color A, ch 20 or even number of chs, pull up lp in 2nd ch from hook, pull up lp in each ch across, turn. *(20 lps on hook)*

Row 2: With color B, pull through 1 lp on hook, *ch 1, yo, pull through 3 lps on hook *(completes ch-2 and a

shell)*, rep from* across to last 2 lps on hook, yo, pull through last 2 lps on hook, **do not turn**.

Row 3: Ch 1, sk first vertical bar, **sc lp** *(see Special Stitch)* in top strand of next **horizontal bar** *(see illustration)*, sc lp in next ch sp, 2 sc lps in each ch sp across, 2 sc lps in sp under last horizontal bar, turn.

Horizontal Bar

Row 4: With color A, rep row 2.

Row 5: Ch 1, sk first vertical bar, sk all shells, pull up lp in top strand of each ch or horizontal bar across, turn.

Rows 6–24: [Rep rows 2–5 consecutively] 5 times, ending last rep with row 4.

Row 25: Ch 1, sk first vertical bar, sl st in top strand of each horizontal bar across. Fasten off. ■

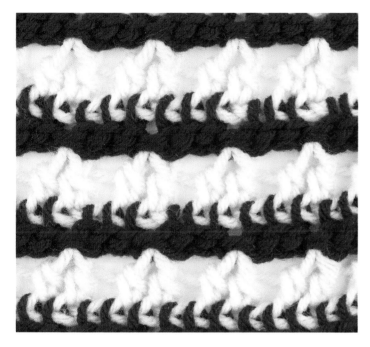

MATERIALS

- Medium (worsted) weight yarn:
  1 oz/50 yds/28g 2 colors A and B
- Size K/10½/6.5mm double-ended hook
  used for photographed block

4 MEDIUM

PATTERN NOTES

Read General Instructions on pages 5–7 before beginning pattern.

Chain-2 at beginning of row or round counts as first double crochet loop unless otherwise stated.

SPECIAL STITCH

Double crochet loop (dc lp): Yo, pull up lp in next st, yo, pull through 2 lps on hook.

INSTRUCTIONS

STITCH PATTERN

Row 1: With color A, ch 21 or in multiples of 3 chs, pull up lp in 2nd ch from hook, pull up lp in each ch across, turn. *(21 lps on hook)*

Row 2: With color B, work lps off, **do not turn**.

Row 3: Ch 2 *(see Pattern Notes)*, sk next **horizontal bar** *(see illustration)*, **dc lp** *(see Special Stitch)* in top strand of each of next 2 horizontal bars, sk next horizontal bar, [dc lp in top strand of each of next 2 horizontal bars, sk next horizontal bar] across to last horizontal bar, dc lp in top strand of last horizontal bar, turn. *(14 lps on hook)*

Horizontal Bar

Row 4: With color A, pull through first lp on hook, *ch 2, pull through 3 lps on hook *(completes a ch-3 and a shell)*, rep from * across to last 2 lps on hook, ch 1, yo, pull through last 2 lps on hook *(completes a ch-2 and a vertical bar)*, **do not turn**.

Row 5: Ch 1, sk first vertical bar, pull up lp in top strand of each ch across, turn. *(21 lps on hook)*

Rows 6–20: [Rep rows 2–5 consecutively] 4 times, ending last rep with row 4.

Row 21: Ch 1, sk first vertical bar, sl st in top strand of each ch across. Fasten off. ■

design by Dorris Brooks

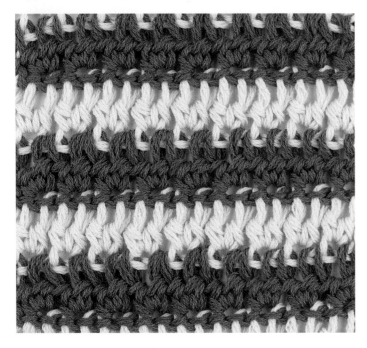

MATERIALS

- Medium (worsted) weight yarn:
  1 oz/50 yds/28g 2 colors A and B
- Size H/8/5mm double-ended hook used
  for photographed block

4 MEDIUM

PATTERN NOTES

Read General Instructions on pages 5–7 before beginning pattern.

Work in space under horizontal bar unless otherwise indicated.

SPECIAL STITCHES

Single crochet loop (sc lp): Pull up lp in place indicated, ch 1.

Double crochet loop (dc lp): Yo, pull up lp in indicated place, yo, pull through 2 lps on hook.

INSTRUCTIONS

STITCH PATTERN

Row 1: With color A, ch 20 or even number of chs, 2 **dc lps** (see Special Stitches) in 3rd ch from hook, [sk next ch, 2 dc lp in next ch] across to last ch, **sc lp** (see Special Stitches) in last ch, turn. (20 lps on hook)

Row 2: With color B, work lps off hook, **do not turn**.

Row 3: Ch 1, sk first **horizontal bar** (see illustration), 2 dc lps in next horizontal bar, [sk next horizontal bar, 2 dc lps in next horizontal bar] across to last horizontal bar, sc lp in last horizontal bar, turn.

Horizontal Bar

Rows 4 & 5: With color A, rep rows 2 and 3.

Rows 6–16: [Rep rows 2–5 consecutively] 3 times, ending last row with row 4.

Row 17: Ch 2, sk next horizontal bar, 2 dc in next horizontal bar, [sk next horizontal bar, 2 dc in next horizontal bar] across to last horizontal bar, sc in last horizontal bar. Fasten off. ■

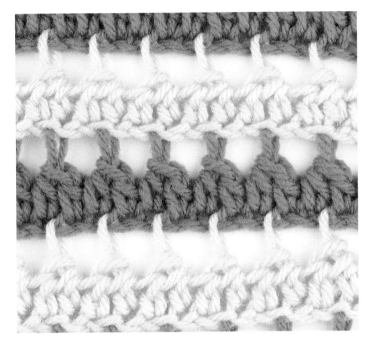

MATERIALS
- Medium (worsted) weight yarn:
  1 oz/50 yds/28g 2 colors A and B
- Size K/10½/6.5mm double-ended hook
  used for photographed block

4 MEDIUM

PATTERN NOTES
Read General Instructions on pages 5–7 before beginning pattern.

Chain-2 at beginning of row or round counts as first double crochet loop unless otherwise stated.

SPECIAL STITCHES
Half double crochet cluster (hdc cl): Yo, pull up lp in place indicated, yo, pull through 2 lps on hook, yo, pull up lp in next place indicated, [yo, pull through 2 lps on hook] twice.

Double crochet loop (dc lp): Yo, pull up lp in place indicated, yo, pull through 2 lps on hook.

INSTRUCTIONS
STITCH PATTERN
Row 1: With color A, ch 21 or in multiples of 2 plus 1 ch, **hdc cl** (see Special Stitches) in 3rd and 4th chs

from hook, hdc cl across to last ch, **dc lp** (see Special Stitches) in last ch, turn. (11 lps on hook)

Row 2: With color B, pull through first lp on hook, *ch 1, yo, pull through 2 lps on hook (completes a ch-2 and vertical bar), rep from * across to last 2 lps on hook, yo, pull through last 2 lps on hook, **do not turn**.

Row 3: Ch 2 (see Pattern Notes), working in top strand of each ch across, hdc cl in top strand of next **horizontal bar** (see illustration) and in first ch, hdc cl in next 2 chs across to last ch, dc lp in last ch, turn.

Horizontal Bar

Rows 4 & 5: With color A, rep rows 2 and 3.

Rows 6–9: Rep rows 2–5. At end of last row, **do not turn**.

Row 10: With color A, pull through first lp on hook, [ch 1, yo, pull through 2 lps on hook] across. Fasten off. ∎

design by Dorris Brooks

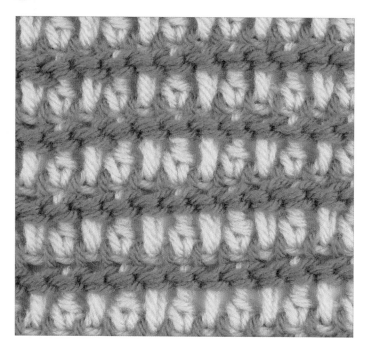

MATERIALS
- Medium (worsted) weight yarn:
  1 oz/50 yds/28g 2 colors A and B
- Size K/10½/6.5mm double-ended hook
  used for photographed block

4 MEDIUM

PATTERN NOTE
Read General Instructions on pages 5–7 before beginning pattern.

SPECIAL STITCH
Double crochet loop (dc lp): Yo, pull up lp in place indicated, yo, pull through 2 lps on hook.

INSTRUCTIONS
STITCH PATTERN
Row 1: With color A, ch 21 or in multiples of 2 plus 1 chs, pull up lp in 2nd ch from hook, pull up lp in each ch across, turn. *(21 lps on hook)*

Row 2: With color B, work lps off hook, **do not turn.**

Row 3: Ch 1, **dc lp** *(see Special Stitch)* in top strand of first **horizontal bar** *(see illustration)*, pull up lp in top strand of next horizontal bar, [dc lp in top strand of next horizontal bar, pull up lp in top strand of next horizontal bar] across, turn.

Horizontal Bar

Row 4: With color A, work lps off hook, **do not turn.**

Row 5: Ch 1, pull up lp in top strand of each horizontal bar across, turn.

Rows 6–28: [Rep rows 2–5 consecutively] 6 times, ending last rep with row 4.

Row 29: Ch 1, sc in each horizontal bar across. Fasten off. ∎

design by Darla Fanton

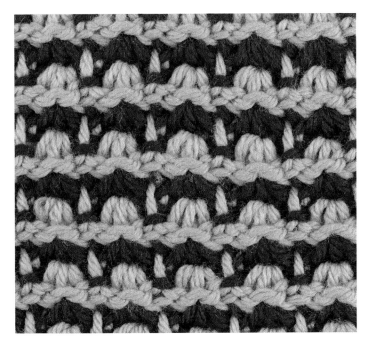

MATERIALS
- Medium (worsted) weight yarn:
  1 oz/50 yds/28g each 2 colors A and B
- Size K/10½/6.5mm double-ended hook
  used for photographed block

4 MEDIUM

PATTERN NOTE
Read General Instructions on pages 5–7 before beginning pattern.

SPECIAL STITCH
Shell: Yo, pull through 4 lps on hook.

INSTRUCTIONS
STITCH PATTERN
Row 1: With color A, ch 37 or in multiples of 4 plus 1 ch, pull up lp in 2nd ch from hook, pull up lp in each ch across, turn. *(37 lps on hook)*

Row 2: With color B, pull through first lp on hook, [**shell** *(see Special Stitch)*, yo, pull through 2 lps on hook] across, **do not turn.** *(10 lps, 9 shells)*

Row 3: Ch 1, pull up lp in top strand of first **horizontal bar** *(see illustration)*, pull up lp in top of next shell, pull up lp in top strand of next horizontal bar, pull up lp in next vertical bar, [pull up lp in top strand of next horizontal bar, pull up lp in top of next shell, pull up lp in top strand of next horizontal bar, pull up lp in next vertical bar] across, turn.

Horizontal Bar

Rows 4 & 5: With color A, rep rows 2 and 3.

Rows 6–36: [Rep rows 2–5 consecutively] 8 times, ending last rep with row 4.

Row 37: Ch 1, [sl st in top strand of next horizontal bar, sl st in next shell, sl st in top strand of next horizontal bar, sl st in next vertical bar] across. Fasten off. ■

design by Darla Fanton

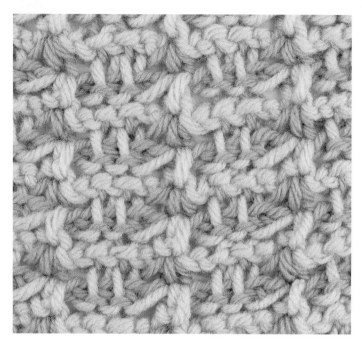

MATERIALS
- Medium (worsted) weight yarn:
  1 oz/50 yds/28g each 2 colors A and B
- Size K/10½/6.5mm double-ended hook
  used for photographed block

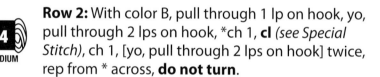

4 MEDIUM

PATTERN NOTE
Read General Instructions on pages 5–7 before beginning pattern.

SPECIAL STITCH
Cluster (cl): Pull through 4 lps on hook.

INSTRUCTIONS
STITCH PATTERN
Row 1: With color A, ch 26 or in multiples of 5 plus 1 chs, pull up lp in 2nd ch from hook, [yo, sk next ch, pull up lp in next ch, yo, sk next ch, pull up lp in next 2 chs] across, turn. (26 lps on hook)

Row 2: With color B, pull through 1 lp on hook, yo, pull through 2 lps on hook, *ch 1, **cl** (see Special Stitch), ch 1, [yo, pull through 2 lps on hook] twice, rep from * across, **do not turn**.

Row 3: Sk first vertical bar, pull up lp in next vertical bar, *yo, pull up lp in top of next cl, yo, [pull up lp in next vertical bar] twice, rep from * across, turn.

Rows 4 & 5: With color A, rep rows 2 and 3.

Rows 6–36: [Rep rows 2–5 consecutively] 8 times, ending last rep with row 4.

Row 37: Ch 1, sk first vertical bar, sl st in next vertical bar, *ch 1, sl st in top of next cluster, ch 1, [sl st in next vertical bar] twice, rep from * across. Fasten off. ■

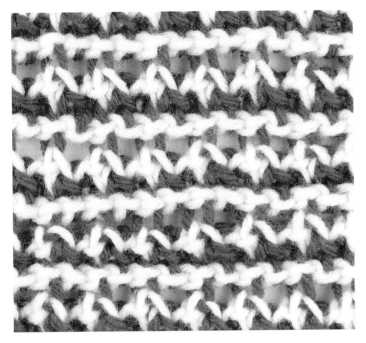

MATERIALS
- Medium (worsted) weight yarn:
  1 oz/50 yds/28g 2 colors A and B
- Size K/10½/6.5mm double-ended hook
  used for photographed block

4 MEDIUM

PATTERN NOTE
Read General Instructions on pages 5–7 before beginning pattern.

SPECIAL STITCH
Single crochet loop (sc lp): Insert hook in place indicated, yo, pull lp through, yo, pull through 1 lp on hook.

INSTRUCTIONS
STITCH PATTERN
Row 1: With color A, ch 27 or odd number of chs, pull up lp in 2nd ch from hook, pull up lp in each ch across, turn. *(27 lps on hook)*

Row 2: With color B, work lps off hook, **do not turn**.

Row 3: Ch 1, sk first vertical bar, yo, sk next vertical bar, **sc lp** *(see Special Stitch)* in next vertical bar, [yo, sk next vertical bar, sc lp in next vertical bar] across, turn.

Row 4: With color A, work lps off hook, **do not turn**.

Row 5: Ch 1, sk first vertical bar, [sc lp in lower right-hand strand of next vertical bar, sk upper strand of same bar, pull up lp in next vertical bar] across, turn.

Rows 6–32: [Rep rows 2–5 consecutively] 7 times, ending last rep with row 4.

Row 33: Ch 1, sk first vertical bar, [sc lp in lower right-hand strand of next vertical bar, yo, pull through 2 lps on hook, sk upper strand of same bar, sl st in next vertical bar] across. Fasten off. ∎

design by Jennifer McClain

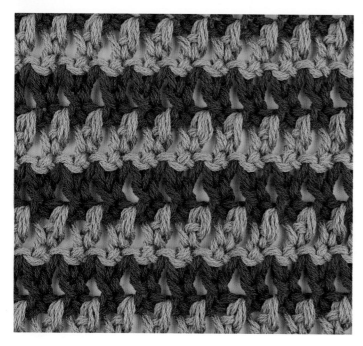

MATERIALS
- Medium (worsted) weight yarn:
  1 oz/50 yds/28g 2 colors A and B
- Size H/8/5mm double-ended hook used
  for photographed block

4 MEDIUM

PATTERN NOTE
Read General Instructions on pages 5–7 before beginning pattern.

SPECIAL STITCH
Single crochet loop (sc lp): Pull up lp in place indicated, ch 1.

INSTRUCTIONS
STITCH PATTERN
Row 1: With color A, ch 28 or even number of chs, **sc lp** *(see Special Stitch)* in 2nd ch from hook, [yo, sk next ch, sc lp in next ch] across, turn. *(28 lps on hook)*

Row 2: With color B, pull through first lp on hook, [ch 1, yo, pull through 3 lps on hook *(completes 2 chs and vertical bar)*] across to last 2 lps on hook, yo, pull through last 2 lps on hook, **do not turn.**

Row 3: Ch 1, sk first vertical bar, sc lp in top strand of next **horizontal bar** *(see illustration)*, [yo, sk next ch, sc lp in top strand of next ch] across, turn.

Horizontal Bar

Rows 4 & 5: With color A, rep rows 2 and 3.

Rows 6–20: [Rep rows 2–5 consecutively] 4 times, ending last rep with row 4.

Row 21: Ch 1, sk first vertical bar, sc in next horizontal bar, [sk next ch, 2 sc in top strand of next ch] across. Fasten off. ■

number 80

design by Dorris Brooks

MATERIALS

- Medium (worsted) weight yarn:
  1 oz/50 yds/28g 2 colors A and B
- Size H/8/5mm double-ended hook used
  for photographed block

4 MEDIUM

PATTERN NOTES

Read General Instructions on pages 5–7 before beginning pattern.

Chain-2 at beginning and end of row counts as first and last stitch unless otherwise stated.

SPECIAL STITCH

Double crochet loop (dc lp): Yo, pull up lp in place indicated, yo, pull through 2 lps on hook.

INSTRUCTIONS

STITCH PATTERN

Row 1: With color A, ch 20 or in multiples of 3 plus 2 chs, pull up lp in 2nd ch from hook, pull up lp in each ch across, turn. *(20 lps on hook)*

Row 2: With color B, work lps off hook, **do not turn**.

Row 3: Ch 2 *(see Pattern Notes)*, sk next **horizontal bar** *(see illustration)*, 3 **dc lps** *(see Special Stitch)* in top strand of next horizontal bar, [sk next 2 horizontal bars, 3 dc lps in top strand of next horizontal bar] across to last 2 horizontal bars, sk next horizontal bar, pull up lp in top strand of last horizontal bar, **ch 2** *(see Pattern Notes)*, turn.

Horizontal Bar

Row 4: With color A, work lps off hook, **do not turn**.

Row 5: Ch 1, sk first vertical bar, pull up lp in top strand of each horizontal bar across, turn.

Rows 6–20: [Rep rows 2–5 consecutively] 4 times, ending last rep with row 4.

Row 21: Ch 1, sk first vertical bar, sl st in top strand of each horizontal bar across. Fasten off. ■

design by Dorris Brooks

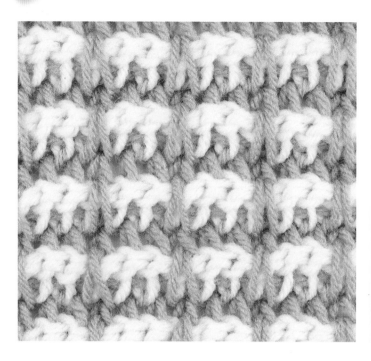

MATERIALS

- Medium (worsted) weight yarn:
  1 oz/50 yds/28g 2 colors A and B
- Size K/10½/6.5mm double-ended hook
  used for photographed block

4 MEDIUM

PATTERN NOTE

Read General Instructions on pages 5–7 before beginning pattern.

SPECIAL STITCH

Spike stitch (spike st): Working around last 3 rows, insert hook from front to back through center of corresponding vertical bar 4 rows below, yo, pull up long lp, ch 1, sk next horizontal bar on last row behind spike st.

INSTRUCTIONS

STITCH PATTERN

Row 1: With color A, ch 21 or in multiples of 3 chs, pull up lp in 2nd ch from hook, pull up lp in each ch across, turn. *(21 lps on hook)*

Row 2: With color B, work lps off hook, **do not turn.**

Row 3: Ch 1, sk first vertical bar, pull up lp in top strand of each **horizontal bar** *(see illustration)* across, turn.

Horizontal Bar

Row 4: With color B, work lps off hook, **do not turn.**

Row 5: Ch 1, sk first vertical bar, **spike st** *(see Special Stitch)* in 2nd vertical bar 4 rows below, [pull up lp in top strand of next 2 horizontal bars, spike st] across to last horizontal bar, pull up lp in top strand of last horizontal bar, turn.

Rows 6–28: [Rep rows 2–5 consecutively] 6 times, ending last rep with row 4.

Row 29: Ch 1, sc in top strand of each horizontal bar and in each spike st across. Fasten off. ∎

design by Dorris Brooks

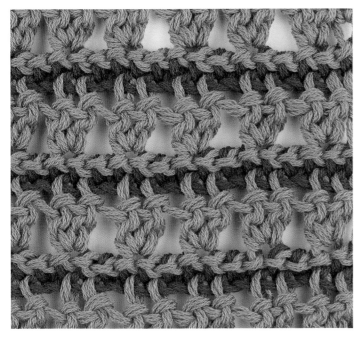

MATERIALS

- Medium (worsted) weight yarn:
  1 oz/50 yds/28g 2 colors A and B
- Size H/8/5mm double-ended hook used
  for photographed block

4 MEDIUM

PATTERN NOTE

Read General Instructions on pages 5–7 before beginning pattern.

SPECIAL STITCH

Double crochet loop (dc lp): Yo, pull up lp in next st, yo, pull through 2 lps on hook.

INSTRUCTIONS

STITCH PATTERN

Row 1: With color A, ch 20 or in multiples of 3 plus 2 chs, pull up lp in 2nd ch from hook, pull up lp in each ch across, turn. *(20 lps on hook)*

Row 2: With color B, work lps off hook, **do not turn**.

Row 3: Ch 2, sk next **horizontal bar** *(see illustration)*, (**dc lp**—*see Special Stitch*, ch 1) twice in top strand of next horizontal bar, [sk next 2 horizontal bars, (dc lp, ch 1) twice in top strand of next horizontal bar] across to last 2 horizontal bars, sk next horizontal bar, pull up lp in last horizontal bar, ch 1, turn.

Horizontal Bar

Row 4: With color A, pull through first lp on hook, *ch 1, [yo, pull through 2 lps on hook] twice, rep from * across to last 2 lps on hook, yo, pull through last 2 lps on hook, **do not turn**.

Row 5: Ch 1, sk first vertical bar, pull up lp in top strand of each horizontal bar and ch across, turn.

Rows 6–16: [Rep rows 2–5 consecutively] 3 times, ending last rep with row 4.

Row 17: Ch 1, sk first vertical bar, sl st in top strand of each horizontal bar and ch across. Fasten off. ∎

design by Dorris Brooks

MATERIALS
- Medium (worsted) weight yarn:
  1 oz/50 yds/28g 2 colors A and B
- Size H/8/5mm double-ended hook used
  for photographed block

4 MEDIUM

PATTERN NOTE
Read General Instructions on pages 5–7 before
beginning pattern.

SPECIAL STITCH
Double crochet loop (dc lp): Yo, pull up lp in next st,
yo, pull through 2 lps on hook.

INSTRUCTIONS
STITCH PATTERN
Row 1: With color A, ch 21 or in multiples of 3 chs,
(**dc lp**—*see Special Stitch*, ch 1) twice in 4th ch from
hook, [sk next 2 chs, (dc lp, ch 1) twice in next ch]
across to last 2 chs, sk next ch, pull up lp in last ch,
ch 1, turn. *(14 lps on hook)*

Row 2: With color B, pull through first lp on hook,
*ch 1, [yo, pull through 2 lps on hook] twice, rep
from * across to last 2 lps on hook, yo, pull through
last 2 lps on hook, **do not turn**.

Row 3: Ch 2, sk next **horizontal bar**
(see illustration), (dc lp, ch 1) twice in top
strand of next horizontal bar, *sk next 2
chs, (dc lp, ch 1) twice in next horizontal
bar, rep from * across to last 2 chs,
sk next horizontal bar, pull up lp in last horizontal
bar, ch 2, turn.

Horizontal Bar

Rows 4 & 5: With color A, rep rows 2 and 3.

Rows 6–13: [Rep rows 2–5 consecutively] twice.
At end of last row, **do not turn**.

Row 14: With color A, work lps off hook.

Row 15: Ch 1, sk first vertical bar, sl st in each
horizontal bar across. Fasten off. ■

design by Darla Fanton

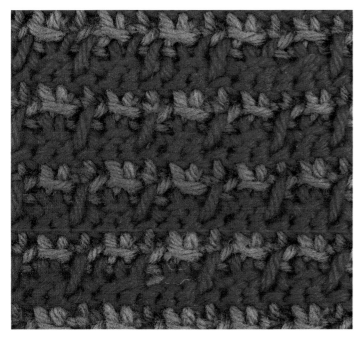

MATERIALS

- Medium (worsted) weight yarn:
  1 oz/50 yds/28g each 2 colors A and B
- Size K/10½/6.5mm double-ended hook
  used for photographed block

4 MEDIUM

PATTERN NOTE

Read General Instructions on pages 5–7 before beginning pattern.

INSTRUCTIONS

STITCH PATTERN

Row 1: With color A, ch 29 or in multiples of 3 plus 2 chs, pull up lp in 2nd ch from hook, pull up lp in each ch across, turn. *(29 lps on hook)*

Row 2: With color B, work lps off hook, **do not turn**.

Row 3: Ch 1, sk first vertical bar, *yo, pull up lp in top strand in each of next 3 **horizontal bars** *(see illustration)*, pick up first st of last 3-st group and bring off hook over last 2 lps, rep from * across to last horizontal bar, pull up lp in top strand of last horizontal bar, turn.

Horizontal Bar

Rows 4 & 5: With color A, rep rows 2 and 3.

Rows 6–32: [Rep rows 2–5 consecutively] 7 times, ending last rep with row 4.

Row 33: Ch 1, sl st in top strand of each horizontal bar across. Fasten off. ■

design by Dorris Brooks

MATERIALS
- Medium (worsted) weight yarn:
  1 oz/50 yds/28g 2 colors A and B
- Size H/8/5mm double-ended hook used
  for photographed block

4 MEDIUM

PATTERN NOTE
Read General Instructions on pages 5–7 before beginning pattern.

SPECIAL STITCH
Double crochet loop (dc lp): Yo, pull up lp in next st, yo, pull through 2 lps on hook.

INSTRUCTIONS
STITCH PATTERN

Row 1: With color A, ch 23 or in multiples of 2 plus 1 chs, **dc lp** *(see Special Stitch)* in 4th ch from hook, dc lp in each ch across, turn. *(21 lps on hook)*

Row 2: With color B, pull through 1 lp on hook, [yo, pull through 2 lps on hook] across, **do not turn**.

Row 3: Ch 2, sk next **horizontal bar** *(see illustration)*, [dc lp in top strand of next horizontal bar, sk next horizontal bar] across to last horizontal bar, pull up lp in top strand of last horizontal bar, ch 2, turn.

Horizontal Bar

Row 4: With color A, pull through first lp on hook, [ch 1, yo, pull through 2 lps on hook] across, **do not turn**.

Row 5: Ch 2, dc lp in each horizontal bar and in each ch across, turn.

Rows 6–12: [Rep rows 2–5 consecutively] twice, ending last rep with row 4.

Row 13: Ch 2, sk first vertical bar, hdc in each horizontal bar across. Fasten off. ■

design by Darla Fanton

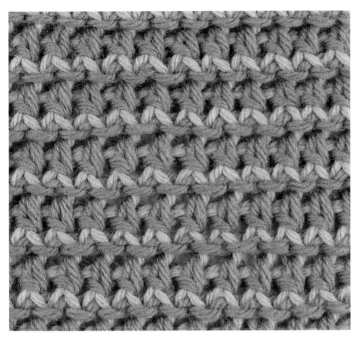

MATERIALS
- Medium (worsted) weight yarn:
  1 oz/50 yds/28g each 2 colors A and B
- Size K/10½/6.5mm double-ended hook
  used for photographed block

4 MEDIUM

PATTERN NOTE
Read General Instructions on pages 5–7 before beginning pattern.

INSTRUCTIONS
STITCH PATTERN
Row 1: With color A, ch 35 or odd number of chs, pull up lp in 2nd ch from hook, pull up lp in each ch across, turn. *(35 lps on hook)*

Row 2: With color B, pull through 1 lp on hook, [yo, pull through 3 lps on hook] across, **do not turn**.

Row 3: Yo, sk first vertical bar, pull up lp in next 2 vertical bars at same time, [yo, pull up lp in next 2 vertical bars at same time] across, turn.

Rows 4 & 5: With color A, rep rows 2 and 3.

Rows 6–40: [Rep rows 2–5 consecutively] 9 times, ending last rep with row 4.

Row 41: Yo, sk first vertical bar, pull up lp in next 2 vertical bars at same time, yo, pull through all 3 lps on hook, [yo, pull up lp in next 2 vertical bars at same time, yo, pull through all 3 lps on hook] across. Fasten off. ■

design by Dorris Brooks

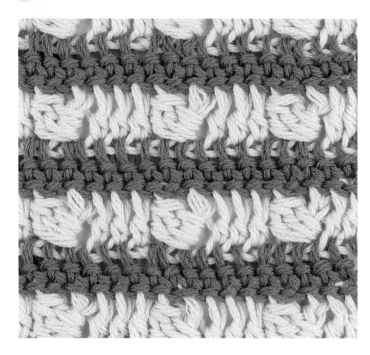

MATERIALS
- Medium (worsted) weight yarn:
  1 oz/50 yds/28g 2 colors A and B
- Size H/8/5mm double-ended hook used
  for photographed block

4 MEDIUM

PATTERN NOTE
Read General Instructions on pages 5–7 before beginning pattern.

SPECIAL STITCHES
Single crochet loop (sc lp): Pull up lp in next ch, ch 1.

Double crochet loop (dc lp): Yo, pull up lp in next st, yo, pull through 2 lps on hook.

Cluster (cl): 3 dc lps around last st worked, yo, pull through 3 lps on hook.

INSTRUCTIONS
STITCH PATTERN
Row 1: With color A, ch 22 or in multiples of 3 plus 1 ch, **sc lp** *(see Special Stitches)* in 3rd ch from hook, sc lp in each ch across, turn. *(21 lps on hook)*

Row 2: With color B, pull through 1 lp on hook, [yo, pull through 2 lps on hook] across, **do not turn**.

Row 3: Ch 2, **dc lp** *(see Special Stitches)* in top stand of next 2 **horizontal bars** *(see illustration)*, sk next horizontal bar, dc lp in next horizontal bar, ch 1, **cl** *(see Special Stitches)*, sk next horizontal bar, [dc lp in top strand of each of next 3 horizontal bars, sk next horizontal bar, dc lp in top strand of next horizontal bar, cl, sk next horizontal bar] across to last 3 horizontal bars, dc lp in top strand of each of next 2 horizontal bars, pull up lp in top strand of last horizontal bar, ch 2, turn. *(18 lps on hook)*

Horizontal Bar

continued on page 110

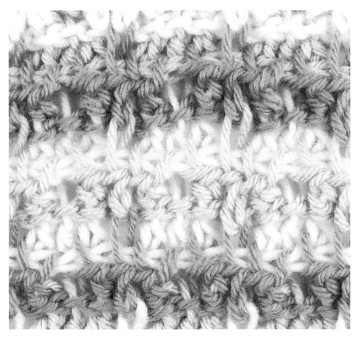

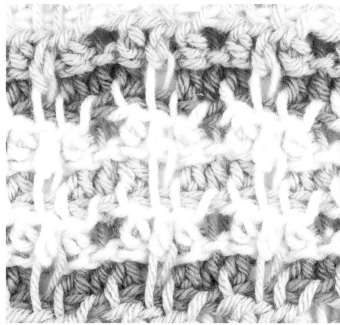

MATERIALS
- Medium (worsted) weight yarn:
  1 oz/50 yds/28g 3 colors A, B and C
- Size K/10½/6.5mm double-ended hook
  used for photographed block

4 MEDIUM

PATTERN NOTE
Read General Instructions on pages 5–7 before beginning pattern.

SPECIAL STITCHES
Double crochet loop (dc lp): Yo, pull up lp in place indicated, yo, pull through 2 lps on hook.

Long double crochet loop (lng dc lp): Yo, pull up long lp in place indicated, yo, pull through 2 lps on hook.

Long half double crochet (lng hdc): Yo, pull up long lp in place indicated, yo, pull through 3 lps on hook.

INSTRUCTIONS
STITCH PATTERN
Row 1: With color A, ch 20 or in multiples of 4 chs, **dc lp** (see Special Stitches) in 3rd ch from hook, dc lp

in next ch, [yo, sk next ch, dc lp in each of next 3 chs] across, turn. (19 lps on hook)

Row 2: With color B, work lps off hook, **do not turn**.

Row 3: Ch 1, sk first vertical bar, yo, sk next vertical bar, dc lp in next vertical bar, *working behind last row, **lng dc lp** (see Special Stitches) in next sk ch on row before last, sk next vertical bar on last row, dc lp in next vertical bar, yo, sk next vertical bar, dc lp in next vertical bar, rep from * across, turn.

Row 4: With color C, work lps off hook, **do not turn**.

Row 5: Ch 1, sk first vertical bar, working behind last row, lng dc lp in sk vertical bar on row before last, sk next vertical bar on last row, dc lp in next vertical bar, *yo, sk next vertical bar, dc lp in next vertical bar, working behind last row, lng dc lp in sk vertical bar on row before last, sk next vertical bar on last row, dc lp in next vertical bar, turn.

Row 6: With color B, work lps off hook, **do not turn**.

continued on page 110

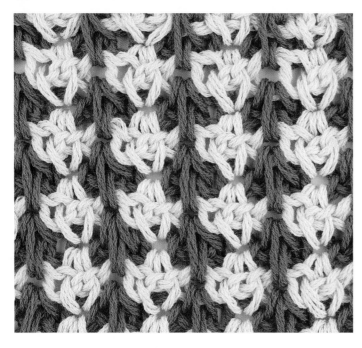

MATERIALS

- Medium (worsted) weight yarn:
  1 oz/50yds/28g 2 colors A and B
- Crochenit hook used for
  photographed block

4 MEDIUM

PATTERN NOTE

Read General Instructions on pages 5–7 before beginning pattern.

SPECIAL STITCH

Corn stitch (corn st): Pull up lp in first ch of next ch-3, insert hook under top strand of 2 **horizontal bars** *(see illustration)* above next shell 3 rows below, yo, pull through, ch 1, pull up lp in last ch of same ch-3.

Horizontal Bar

INSTRUCTIONS

STITCH PATTERN

Row 1: With color A, ch 22 or in multiples of 3 plus 1, pull up lp in 2nd ch from hook, pull up lp in each ch across, turn. *(22 lps on hook)*

Row 2: With color B, pull through 1 lp on hook, yo, pull through 4 lps on hook *(this completes a ch-1 and a shell—see photo A)*, *ch 2, yo, pull through 4 lps on hook *(this completes a ch-3 and a shell—see photo B)*, rep from * across, **do not turn**.

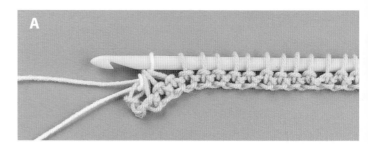

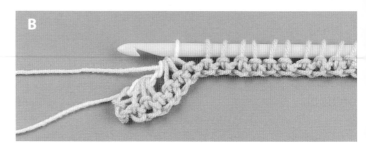

continued on page 110

design by Darla Fanton

MATERIALS
- Medium (worsted) weight yarn:
  1 oz/50 yds/28g each 3 colors *(A, B, and C)*
- Size H/8/5mm double-ended hook used
  for photographed block
- Size H/8/5mm crochet hook

4 MEDIUM

PATTERN NOTE
Read General Instructions on pages 5–7 before
beginning pattern.

SPECIAL STITCHES
Cluster (cl): Yo, pull through 5 lps on hook.

Beginning cluster (beg cl): Pull through first 3 lps
on hook.

End cluster (end cl): Yo, pull through last 4 lps
on hook.

INSTRUCTIONS
STITCH PATTERN
Row 1: With A, ch 38 or in multiples of 18 plus
20, pull up lp in 2nd ch from hook and each ch
across, turn. *(38 lps on hook)*

Row 2: With B, **beg cl** *(see Special Stitches)*, [yo, pull
through 2 lps on hook] 14 times, *cl *(see Special
Stitches)*, [yo, pull through 2 lps on hook] 14 times,
rep from * across to last 4 lps on hook, **end cl** *(see
Special Stitches)*, **do not turn**.

Row 3: Ch 1, sk first cl, pull up lp in
top strand of next **horizontal bar** *(see
illustration)*, pull up lp in top strand
of each of next 6 horizontal bars, (yo,
pull up lp) 4 times in top strand of next
horizontal bar, pull up lp in top strand of each of
next 7 horizontal bars, *sk next cl, pull up lp in top
strand of each of next 7 horizontal bars, (yo, pull
up lp) 4 times in top strand of next horizontal bar,
pull up lp in top strand of each of next 7 horizontal
bars, rep from * across to last cl, pull up lp in top of
last cl, turn.

Horizontal Bar

Row 4: With A, beg cl, [yo, pull through 2 lps on
hook] 7 times, *cl, [yo, pull through 2 lps on hook]
7 times, rep from * across to last 4 lps, end cl,
do not turn.

continued on page 111

design by Jennifer McClain

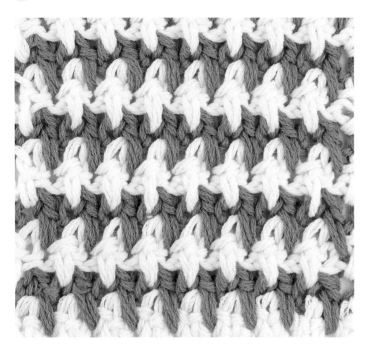

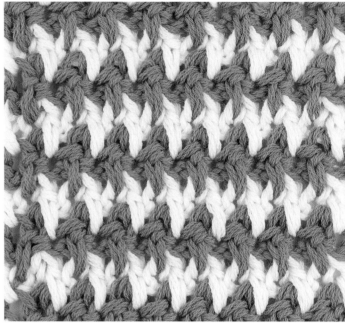

MATERIALS
■ Medium (worsted) weight yarn:
   1 oz/50 yds/28g 2 colors A and B
■ Size H/8/5mm double-ended hook used
   for photographed block

4 MEDIUM

PATTERN NOTE
Read General Instructions on pages 5–7 before beginning pattern.

SPECIAL STITCHES
Single crochet loop (sc lp): Insert hook in next ch, yo, pull lp through, yo, pull through 1 lp on hook.

Long double crochet (lng dc): Yo, insert hook in place indicated, yo, pull up long lp, yo, pull though 2 lps on hook.

INSTRUCTIONS
STITCH PATTERN
Row 1: With color A, ch 20 or even number of chs, **sc lp** (see Special Stitches) in 3rd ch from hook, sc lp in each ch across, turn. (19 lps on hook)

Row 2: With color B, pull through first lp on hook, [ch 1, yo, pull through 3 lps on hook] across, **do not turn**.

Row 3: Ch 1, *working around next **horizontal bar** (see illustration), **lng dc** (see Special Stitches) in same ch on starting ch as corresponding sc lp was worked, pull up lp in top strand of next horizontal bar, rep from * across, turn.

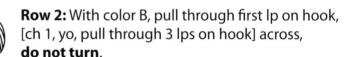

Horizontal Bar

Row 4: With color A, rep row 2.

Row 5: Ch 1, [working over next horizontal bar on last row, long dc in top horizontal strand between sts on row before last, pull up lp in top strand of next horizontal bar on last row] across, turn.

Rows 6–20: Alternating colors B and A, [rep rows 4 and 5 alternately] 8 times, ending last rep with row 4 and color A.

continued on page 111

number 92

design by Sandra Jean Smith

MATERIALS
- Medium (worsted) weight yarn:
  1 oz/50 yds/28g 4 colors (A, B, C and D)
- Size H/8/5mm double-ended hook used
  for photographed block

PATTERN NOTE
Read General Instructions on pages 5–7 before beginning pattern.

INSTRUCTIONS
STITCH PATTERN
Row 1: With A, ch 38 or in multiples of 20 plus 18, pull up lp in 2nd ch from hook and in each ch across, turn. *(38 lps on hook)*

Row 2: With B, work lps off hook, **do not turn**.

Row 3: Ch 2, sk first 2 **horizontal bars** *(see illustration)*, [pull up lp in top strand of next horizontal bar, ch 2] 7 times, pull up lp in next vertical bar, ch 2, pull up lp in top strand of next horizontal bar, ch 2, pull up lp in next vertical bar, ch 2, [pull up lp in top strand of next horizontal bar, ch 2] 8 times,

Horizontal Bar

*sk next 2 horizontal bars, [pull up lp in top strand of next horizontal bar, ch 2] 8 times, pull up lp in next vertical bar, ch 2, pull up lp in top strand of next horizontal bar, ch 2, pull up lp in next vertical bar, ch 2, [pull up lp in top strand of next horizontal bar, ch 2] 8 times, rep from * across, turn.

Row 4: With A, work lps off hook, **do not turn**.

Row 5: Sk first 2 horizontal bars, pull up lp in top strand of each of next 7 horizontal bars, pull up lp in next vertical bar, pull up lp in top stand of next horizontal bar, pull up lp in next vertical bar, pull up lp in top strand of each of next 8 horizontal bars, [sk next 2 horizontal bars, pull up lp in top strand of each of next 8 horizontal bars, pull up lp in next vertical bar, pull up lp in top strand of next horizontal bar, pull up lp in next vertical bar, pull up lp in top strand of each of next 8 horizontal bars] across, turn.

Rows 6 & 7: With C, rep rows 2 and 3.

continued on page 111

design by Jennifer McClain

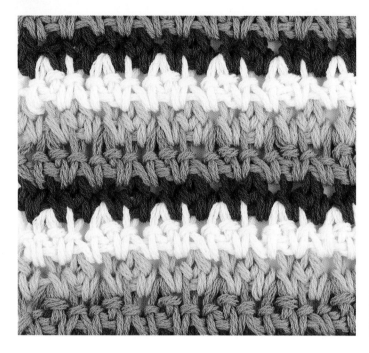

MATERIALS
- Medium (worsted) weight yarn:
  1 oz/50 yds/28g each colors A, B,
  C and D
- Size H/8/5mm double-ended hook used
  for photographed block

4 MEDIUM

PATTERN NOTE
Read General Instructions on page 5–7 before
beginning pattern.

SPECIAL STITCH
Single crochet loop (sc lp): Insert hook in next ch,
yo, pull lp through, yo, pull through 1 lp on hook.

INSTRUCTIONS
STITCH PATTERN
Row 1: With A, ch 22, or in multiples of 3 plus 1, **sc lp**
(see Special Stitch) in 3rd ch from hook, sc lp in each
ch across, turn. *(21 lps on hook)*

Row 2: With B, pull through first lp on hook, yo, pull
through 3 lps on hook, [yo, pull through 2 lps on
hook, yo, pull through 3 lps on hook] across,
do not turn.

Row 3: Ch 1, sc lp in sp under first
horizontal bar *(see illustration)*, sc lp in
next vertical bar, [sc lp in sp under each
of next 2 horizontal bars, sc lp in next
vertical bar] across, turn.

Horizontal Bar

Rows 4–18: Working in color sequence of color
C, color D, Color A, color B, [rep rows 2 and 3
alternately] 8 times, ending with row 2 and color B.

Row 19: Ch 1, sc in sp under first horizontal bar, sc
in next vertical bar, [sc in sp under each of next 2
horizontal bars, sc in next vertical bar] across.
Fasten off. ■

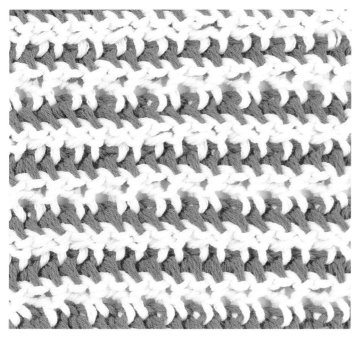

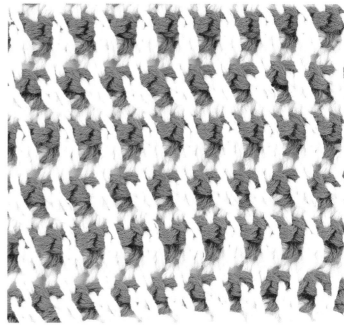

MATERIALS

- Medium (worsted) weight yarn:
  1 oz/50 yds/28g 2 colors A and B
- Size H/8/5mm double-ended hook used
  for photographed block

4 MEDIUM

PATTERN NOTE

Read General Instructions on pages 5–7 before beginning pattern.

SPECIAL STITCHES

Long half double crochet (lng hdc): Yo, pull up lp in place indicated 4 rows below, yo, pull lp through, yo, pull through all 3 lps on hook.

Long double crochet (lng dc): Yo pull up lp in vertical bar of next st 4 rows below, yo, pull lp through, yo, pull through 2 lps on hook.

INSTRUCTIONS

STITCH PATTERN

Row 1: With color A, ch 21 or odd number of chs, pull up lp in 2nd ch from hook, pull up lp in each ch across, turn. *(21 lps on hook)*

Row 2: With color B, work lps off hook, **do not turn**.

Row 3: Ch 1, pull up lp in top strand of first **horizontal bar** *(see illustration)*, pull up lp in top strand of each horizontal bar across, turn.

Horizontal Bar

Row 4: With color A, work lps off hook, **do not turn**.

Row 5: Lng hdc *(see Special Stitches)* in first vertical bar 4 rows below, sk first horizontal bar on last row, pull up lp in top strand of next horizontal bar, *sk next vertical bar 4 rows below, **lng dc** *(see Special Stitches)* in next vertical bar, sk next horizontal bar on last row, pull up lp in top strand of next horizontal bar, rep from * across to last vertical bar, lng dc in last vertical bar 4 rows below, turn.

Rows 6: With color B, work lps off hook, **do not turn.**

Row 7: Ch 1, pull up lp in top strand of first horizontal bar, pull up lp in top strand of each horizontal bar across, turn.

continued on page 112

design by Darla Fanton

MATERIALS
- Medium (worsted) weight yarn:
    1 oz/50 yds/28g 2 colors A and B
- Size H/8/5mm double-ended hook used
    for photographed block

4 MEDIUM

PATTERN NOTE
Read General Instructions on pages 5–7 before beginning pattern.

INSTRUCTIONS
STITCH PATTERN
Row 1: With color A, ch 24 or in multiples of 8, pull up lp in 2nd ch from hook, pull up lp in each ch across, turn. *(24 lps on hook)*

Row 2: With color B, work lps off hook, **do not turn**.

Row 3: Sk first vertical bar, pull up lp in each of next 3 vertical bars, holding yarn in front, pull up lp in top strand in each of next 4 **horizontal bars** *(see illustration)*, [sk next vertical bar, holding

Horizontal Bar

yarn in back, pull up lp in each of next 4 vertical bars, holding yarn in front, pull up lp in top strand of each of next 4 horizontal bars] across, turn.

Row 4: With color A, work lps off hook, **do not turn**.

Row 5: Rep row 3.

Row 6: With color B, work lps off hook, **do not turn**.

Row 7: Sk first horizontal bar, holding yarn in front, pull up lp in top strand of each of next 3 horizontal bars, holding yarn in back, pull up lp in each of next 4 vertical bars, [sk next horizontal bar, holding yarn in front, pull up lp in top strand of next 4 horizontal bars, holding yarn in back, pull up lp in each of next 4 vertical bars] across, turn.

Row 8: With color A, work lps off hook, **do not turn**.

Row 9: Rep row 7.

continued on page 112

design by Jennifer McClain

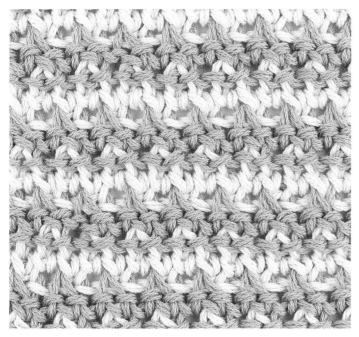

MATERIALS

- Medium (worsted) weight yarn:
  1 oz/50 yds/28g 2 colors A and B
- Size H/8/5mm double-ended hook used
  for photographed block

4 MEDIUM

PATTERN NOTE

Read General Instructions on pages 5–7 before beginning pattern.

SPECIAL STITCH

Single crochet loop (sc lp): Insert hook in place indicated, yo, pull lp through, yo, pull through 1 lp on hook.

INSTRUCTIONS

STITCH PATTERN

Row 1: With color A, ch 20 or even number of chs, **sc lp** (see Special Stitch) in 3rd ch from hook, sc lp in each ch across, turn. *(19 lps on hook)*

Row 2: With color B, work lps off hook, **do not turn**.

Row 3: Ch 1, sc lp in top strand of first **horizontal bar** *(see illustration)*, [insert hook under next 2 vertical bars at same time, yo, pull lp through, yo, pull through 1 lp on hook, sc lp in top strand of next horizontal bar] across to last horizontal bar, sc lp in top strand of last horizontal bar, turn.

Horizontal Bar

Rows 4 & 5: With color A, rep rows 2 and 3.

Row 6: With color B, work lps off hook, **do not turn**.

Row 7: Ch 1, sc lp in top strand of each of first 2 horizontal bars, [insert hook under next 2 vertical bars at same time, yo, pull lp through, yo, pull through 1 lp on hook, sc lp in top strand of next horizontal bar] across, turn.

Row 8: With color A, work lps off hook, **do not turn**.

Row 9: Rep row 7.

continued on page 112

design by Darla Fanton

MATERIALS
- Medium (worsted) weight yarn:
  1 oz/50 yds/28g 2 colors A and B
- Size H/8/5mm double-ended hook used
  for photographed block

4 MEDIUM

PATTERN NOTE
Read General Instructions on pages 5–7 before beginning pattern.

SPECIAL STITCH
Puff stitch (puff st): Yo, pull up lp in next vertical bar of same color 4 rows below, [yo, pull up lp in same bar] twice, yo, pull through 6 lps on hook, ch 1.

INSTRUCTIONS
STITCH PATTERN
Row 1: With color A, ch 23 or in multiples of 8 plus 7 chs, pull up lp in 2nd ch from hook, pull up lp in each ch across, turn. *(23 lps on hook)*

Row 2: With color B, work lps off hook, **do not turn**.

Row 3: Ch 1, pull up lp in top strand of each **horizontal bar** *(see illustration)* across, turn.

Horizontal Bar

Row 4: With color A, work lps off hook, **do not turn**.

Row 5: Ch 1, pull up lp in top strand of each of first 6 horizontal bars, ***puff st** (see Special Stitch)*, sk next horizontal bar, pull up lp in top strand of each of next 7 horizontal bars, rep from * across, turn.

Row 6: With color B, work lps off hook, **do not turn**.

Row 7: Ch 1, pull up lp in top strand of each of first 2 horizontal bars, puff st, sk next horizontal bar, [pull up lp in top strand of each of next 7 horizontal bars, puff st, sk next horizontal bar] across to last 3 horizontal bars, pull up lp in top strand of each of last 3 horizontal bars, turn.

Row 8: With color A, work lps off hook, **do not turn**.

Row 9: Rep row 7.

continued on page 112

design by Dorris Brooks

MATERIALS
- Medium (worsted) weight yarn:
  1 oz/50 yds/28g 2 colors A and B
- K/10½/6.5mm double-ended hook used
  for photographed block

4 MEDIUM

PATTERN NOTE
Read General Instructions on pages 5–7 before beginning pattern.

SPECIAL STITCH
Long double crochet post stitch (lng dc post):
Yo, insert hook around both strands of indicated vertical bar 4 rows below, yo, pull lp through, yo, pull through 1 lp on hook, yo, pull through 2 lps on hook, yo, pull through 1 lp on hook. Sk horizontal bar on last row behind post st.

INSTRUCTIONS
STITCH PATTERN
Row 1: With color A, ch 22 or in multiples of 5 plus 2, pull up lp in 2nd ch from hook, pull up lp in each ch across, turn. *(22 lps on hook)*

Row 2: With color B, work lps off hook, **do not turn**.

Row 3: Ch 1, pull up lp in top strand of each **horizontal bar** *(see illustration)* across, turn.

Horizontal Bar

Row 4: With color A, work lps off hook, **do not turn**.

Row 5: Ch 1, pull up lp in top strand of each horizontal bar across, turn.

Row 6: With color B, work lps off hook, **do not turn**.

Row 7: Lng dc post *(see Special Stitch)* around 4th vertical bar 4 rows below, pull up lp in top strand of next 3 horizontal bars on last row, *lng dc post around same vertical bar 4 rows below, sk next 4 vertical bars 4 rows below, lng dc post around next vertical bar, pull up lp in top strand of next 3 horizontal bars on last row, rep from * across to last 2 horizontal bars on last row, lng dc post around same vertical bar 4 rows below, pull up lp in last horizontal bar, turn.

Row 8: With color A, work lps off hook, **do not turn**.

continued on page 113

design by Dorris Brooks

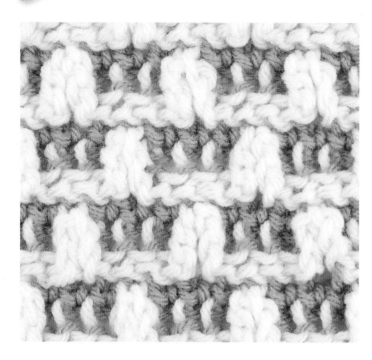
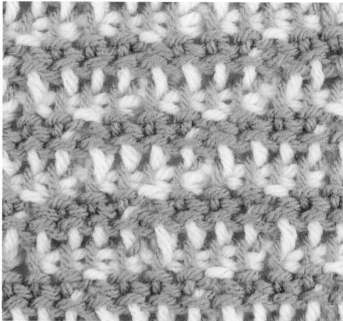

MATERIALS
- Medium (worsted) weight yarn:
  1 oz/50 yds/28g 2 colors A and B
- Size K/10½/6.5mm double-ended hook
  used for photographed block

4 MEDIUM

PATTERN NOTE
Read General Instructions on pages 5–7 before beginning pattern.

SPECIAL STITCH
Single crochet loop (sc lp): Pull up lp in place indicated, ch 1.

INSTRUCTIONS
STITCH PATTERN

Row 1: With color A, ch 21 or in multiples of 4 plus 1, **sc lp** *(see Special Stitch)* in 2nd ch from hook, sc lp in each ch across, turn. *(21 lps on hook)*

Row 2: With B, pull through 1 lp on hook, yo, pull through 2 lps on hook, ch 6, *[yo, pull through 2 lps on hook] 4 times, ch 6, rep from * 3 times, [yo, pull through 2 lps on hook] 3 times, **do not turn.**

Row 3: Ch 1, sk first vertical bar, sk all ch lps, pull up lp in each vertical bar across, turn.

Row 4: With color A, pull through 1 lp on hook, [yo, pull through 2 lps on hook] across, **do not turn.**

Row 5: Ch 1, sk first vertical bar, sc lp in top strand of next **horizontal bar** *(see illustration)*, pull up lp in center ch of next ch lp on row before last, sk next horizontal bar on last row, *sc lp in top strand of each of next 3 horizontal bars, pull up lp in center ch of next ch lp on row before last, sk next horizontal bar on last row; rep from * 3 times, sc lp in top strand of each of last 2 horizontal bars, turn.

Horizontal Bar

Row 6: With color B, pull through 1 lp on hook, [yo, pull through 2 lps on hook] 3 times, ch 6, *[yo, pull through 2 lps on hook] 4 times, ch 6, rep from * twice, [yo, pull through 2 lps on hook] 5 times, **do not turn.**

Row 7: Ch 1, sk first vertical bar, sk all ch lps, pull up lp in each vertical bar across, turn.

continued on page 113

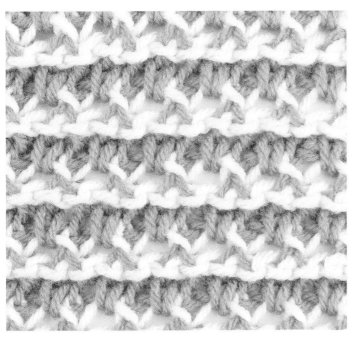

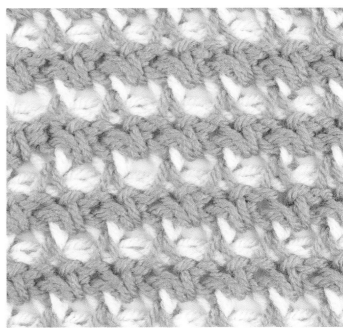

MATERIALS
- Medium (worsted) weight yarn:
  1 oz/50 yds/28g 2 colors A and B
- Size K/10½/6.5mm double-ended hook
  used for photographed block

4 MEDIUM

PATTERN NOTE
Read General Instructions on pages 5–7 before beginning pattern.

SPECIAL STITCH
Single crochet loop (sc lp): Pull up lp in place indicated, ch 1.

INSTRUCTIONS
STITCH PATTERN
Row 1: With color A, ch 20 or even number of chs, **sc lp** *(see Special Stitch)* in 2nd ch from hook, sc lp in each ch across, turn. *(20 lps on hook)*

Row 2: With color B, work lps off hook, **do not turn.**

Row 3: Ch 1, sk 1 vertical bar, [pull up lp in next 2 vertical bars at same time] across to last vertical bar, pull up lp in last vertical bar, turn. *(11 lps on hook)*

Row 4: With color A, pull through first lp on hook, [ch 2, pull through 2 lps on hook] across to last 2 lps on hook, ch 1, pull through last 2 lps, **do not turn.**

Row 5: Ch 1, sc lp in top strand of next **horizontal bar** *(see illustration)*, ch 1, insert hook in first long horizontal strand on row before last and in next ch sp on last row at same time, yo, pull lp through, ch 1, pull up lp in last ch of same ch sp, [insert hook in next long horizontal strand on row before last and in next ch sp on last row at same time, yo, pull lp through, ch 1, pull up lp in last ch of same ch sp] across, turn.

Horizontal Bar

Rows 6–28: [Rep rows 2–5 consecutively] 6 times, ending last rep with row 4.

continued on page 113

design by Dorris Brooks

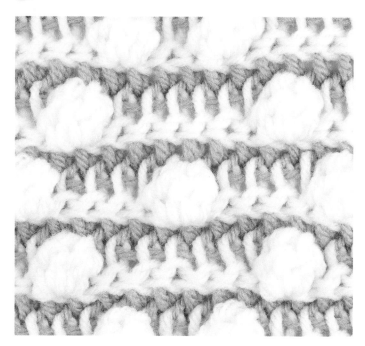

MATERIALS
- Medium (worsted) weight yarn:
  1 oz/50 yds/28g 2 colors A and B
- Size K/10½/6.5mm double-ended hook
  used for photographed block

4 MEDIUM

PATTERN NOTE
Read General Instructions on pages 5–7 before beginning pattern.

SPECIAL STITCH
Bobble: Yo, pull up lp in top strand of next **horizontal bar** *(see illustration)*, yo, pull through 2 lps on hook, [yo, pull up lp in same st, yo, pull through 2 lps on hook] twice, yo, pull through 3 lps on hook.

Horizontal Bar

INSTRUCTIONS
STITCH PATTERN
Row 1: With color A, ch 21 or in multiples of 11 plus 10 chs, pull up lp in 2nd ch from hook, pull up lp in each ch across, turn. *(21 lps on hook)*

Row 2: With color B, work lps off hook, **do not turn.**

Row 3: Ch 1, sk first vertical bar, pull up lp in top strand of each of next 9 horizontal bars, **bobble** *(see Special Stitch)*, pull up lp in top strand of each of last 10 horizontal bars, turn.

Row 4: With color A, work lps off hook, **do not turn.**

Row 5: Ch 1, sk first vertical bar, pull up lp in top strand of each horizontal bar across, turn.

Row 6: With color B, work lps off hook, **do not turn.**

Row 7: Ch 1, sk first vertical bar, pull up lp in top strand in each of next 7 horizontal bars, bobble, pull up lp in top strand in each of next 3 horizontal bars, bobble, pull up lp in top strand in each of last 8 horizontal bars, turn.

Row 8: With color A, work lps off hook, **do not turn.**

Row 9: Ch 1, sk first vertical bar, pull up lp in top strand of each horizontal bar across, turn.

Row 10: With color B, work lps off hook, **do not turn.**

Row 11: Ch 1, sk first vertical bar, pull up lp in top strand in each of next 5 horizontal bars, bobble, pull up lp in top strand in each of next 7 horizontal bars, bobble, pull up lp in top strand in each of last 6 horizontal bars, turn.

Row 12: With color A, work lps off hook, **do not turn**.

Row 13: Ch 1, sk first vertical bar, pull up lp in top strand of each horizontal bar across, turn.

Row 14: With color B, work lps off hook, **do not turn**.

Row 15: Ch 1, sk first vertical bar, pull up lp in top strand in each of next 3 horizontal bars, bobble, [pull up lp in top strand in each of next 5 horizontal bars, bobble] twice, pull up lp in top strand in each of last 4 horizontal bars, turn.

Row 16: With color A, work lps off hook, **do not turn**.

Row 17: Ch 1, sk first vertical bar, pull up lp in top strand of each horizontal bar across, turn.

Row 18: With color B, work lps off hook, **do not turn**.

Row 19: Rep row 11.

Row 20: With color A, work lps off hook, **do not turn**.

Row 21: Ch 1, sk first vertical bar, pull up lp in top strand of each horizontal bar across, turn.

Row 22: With color B, work lps off hook, **do not turn**.

Row 23: Rep row 7.

Row 24: With color A, work lps off hook, **do not turn**.

Row 25: Ch 1, sk first vertical bar, pull up lp in top strand of each horizontal bar across, turn.

Row 26: With color B, work lps off hook, **do not turn**.

Rows 27 & 28: Rep rows 3 and 4.

Row 29: Ch 1, sk first vertical bar, sl st in top strand of each horizontal bar across. Fasten off. ∎

number 87

continued from page 94

Row 4: With color A, pull through first lp on hook, [yo, pull through 2 lps on hook] 3 times, *ch 1, [yo, pull through 2 lps on hook] 5 times, rep from * across to last 5 lps on hook, [yo, pull through 2 lps on hook] 4 times, **do not turn**.

Row 5: Ch 1, sk first vertical bar, sc lp in top strand of each horizontal bar across, turn. *(21 lps on hook)*

Rows 6–16: [Rep rows 2–5 consecutively] 3 times, ending last rep with row 4.

Row 17: Ch 1, sk first vertical bar, sc in top strand of each horizontal bar across. Fasten off. ■

number 88

continued from page 95

Row 7: Ch 1, sk first vertical bar, yo, sk next vertical bar, dc lp in next vertical bar, [working behind last row, lng dc lp in next sk ch on row before last, sk next vertical bar on last row, dc lp in next vertical bar, yo, sk next vertical bar, dc lp in next vertical bar] across, turn.

Row 8: With color A, work lps off hook, **do not turn**.

Row 9: Rep row 5.

Row 10: With color C, work lps off hook, **do not turn**.

Row 11: Rep row 7.

Row 12: With color B, work lps off hook, **do not turn**.

Row 13: Rep row 5.

Row 14: With color C, work lps off hook, **do not turn**.

Row 15: Rep row 7.

Row 16: With color A, work lps off hook, **do not turn**.

Row 17: Rep row 5.

Row 18: With color B, work lps off hook, **do not turn**.

Row 19: Rep row 7.

Rows 20–24: Rep rows 4–8.

Row 25: Ch 1, sc in first vertical bar, working behind last row, **lng hdc** *(see Special Stitches)* in sk vertical bar on row before last, sk corresponding vertical bar on last row, *working in **horizontal bars** *(see illustration)*, sk next vertical bar, sc in top strand of each of next 3 horizontal bars, working behind last row, lng hdc in sk vertical bar on row before last, sk next vertical bar on last row, rep from * across to last horizontal bar, sc in top strand of last horizontal bar. Fasten off. ■

Horizontal Bar

number 89

continued from page 96

Row 3: Ch 1, sk first shell, pull up lp in first ch of next ch-3, insert hook in ch directly below on row 1, yo, pull through, ch 1, pull up lp in last ch of same ch-3 *(this completes a corn st—see photo C)*, *sk next shell, pull up lp in first ch or next ch-3, insert hook in ch directly below on row 1, yo, pull through, ch 1, pull up lp in last ch of same ch-3 *(this completes a corn st)*, rep from * 4 times, sk last shell, pull up lp in last ch, turn. *(20 lps on hook)*

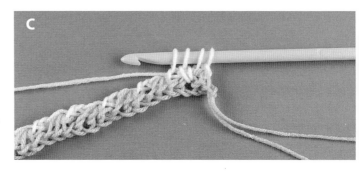

Row 4: With color A, yo, pull through 1 lp on hook, *ch 2, yo, pull through 4 lps on hook (this completes a ch-3 and a shell), rep from * 5 times, ch 2, yo, pull through 2 lps on hook (this completes a ch-3), **do not turn**.

Row 5: Ch 1, **corn st** (see Special Stitch), [sk next shell on this row, corn st] 6 times, turn. (22 lps on hook)

Row 6: With color B, yo, pull through 1 lp on hook, yo, pull through 4 lps on hook (this completes a ch-1 and a shell), *ch 2, yo, pull through 4 lps on hook (this completes a ch-3 and a shell), rep from * across, **do not turn**.

Row 7: Ch 1, sk first shell on this row, corn st, [sk next shell on this row, corn st] 5 times, sk last shell on this row, pull up lp in last ch, turn. (20 lps on hook)

Rows 8–28: [Rep rows 4–7 consecutively] 6 times, ending last rep with row 4.

Row 29: Ch 1, sl st in first ch of next ch-3, insert hook under top strand of 2 horizontal bars above first shell 3 rows below, yo, pull through, yo, pull through 2 lps on hook, sl st in last ch of same ch-3, [sk next shell on this row, sl st in first ch of next ch-3, insert hook under top strand of 2 horizontal bars above next shell 3 rows below, yo, pull through, yo, pull through 2 lps on hook, sl st in last ch of same ch 3] across. Fasten off. ■

number 90
continued from page 97

Row 5: Ch 1, *sk next cl, pull up lp in top strand in each of next 7 horizontal bars, sk next horizontal bar, (yo, pull up lp) 4 times in top of next cl, sk next vertical bar, pull up lp in top strand of each of next 7 horizontal bars, rep from * across to last cl, pull up lp in last cl, turn.

Next rows: Working in color sequence of C, A, B, A, rep rows 4 and 5 alternately, ending with row 4 and A. At end of last row, fasten off. ■

number 91
continued from page 98

Row 21: Ch 1, insert hook under first 2 vertical bars, yo, pull lp through, yo, pull through 2 lps on hook, [working over horizontal bar on last row, hdc under top horizontal strand between sts on row before last, working under both top strands, sc in next horizontal bar] across. Fasten off. ■

number 92
continued from page 99

Rows 8 & 9: Rep rows 4 and 5.

Rows 10 & 11: With D, rep rows 4 and 5.

Rows 12 & 13: Rep rows 4 and 5.

Rows 14 & 15: With C, rep rows 2 and 3.

Rows 16 & 17: Rep rows 4 and 5.

Rows 18 & 19: Rep rows 2 and 3.

Rows 20 & 21: Rep rows 4 and 5.

Rows 22 & 23: With D, rep rows 4 and 5.

Rows 24 & 25: Rep rows 4 and 5.

Next rows: Rep rows 2–25 consecutively, ending with row 21. At end of last row, fasten off. ■

number 94

continued from page 101

Row 8: With color A, work lps off hook, **do not turn**.

Row 9: Sk first vertical bar 4 rows below, lng dc in next vertical bar, sk first horizontal bar of last row, pull up lp in top strand of next horizontal bar, [sk next vertical bar 4 rows below, lng dc in next vertical bar, sk next horizontal bar on last row, pull up lp in top strand of next horizontal bar] across, turn.

Rows 10–28: [Rep rows 2–9 consecutively] 3 times, ending last rep with row 4.

Row 29: Lng hdc in first vertical bar 4 rows below, sk first horizontal bar on last row, sl st in top strand of next horizontal bar, [sk next vertical bar 4 rows below, lng hdc in next vertical bar, sk next horizontal bar on last row, sl st in top strand of next horizontal bar] across to last vertical bar, lng hdc in last vertical bar 4 rows below. Fasten off. ■

number 95

continued from page 102

Rows 10–26: [Rep rows 2–9 consecutively] 3 times, ending last rep with row 2.

Row 27: Sk first vertical bar, sl st in each of next 3 vertical bars, holding yarn in front, sl st in top strand of each of next 4 horizontal bars, [sk next vertical bar, holding yarn in back, sl st in each of next 4 vertical bars, holding yarn in front, sl st in top strand of each of next 4 horizontal bars] across. Fasten off. ■

number 96

continued from page 103

Rows 10–20: [Rep rows 2–9 consecutively] twice, ending last rep with row 4.

Row 21: Ch 1, sc in top strand of first horizontal bar, [insert hook under next 2 vertical bars at same time, yo, pull through, complete as sc, sc in top strand of next horizontal bar] across to last horizontal bar, sc in top strand of last horizontal bar. Fasten off. ■

number 97

continued from page 104

Row 10: With color B, work lps off hook, **do not turn**.

Row 11: Rep row 5.

Rows 12–24: [Rep rows 4–11 consecutively] twice, ending last rep with row 8.

Row 25: Ch 1, sl st in top strand of each of first 2 horizontal bars, puff st, pulling ch-1 through lp on hook, sk next horizontal bar, [sl st in top strand of each of next 7 horizontal bars, puff st, pulling ch-1 through lp on hook, sk next horizontal bar] across to last 3 horizontal bars, sl st in each of last 3 horizontal bars. Fasten off. ■

number 98
continued from page 105

Row 9: Ch 1, pull up lp in top strand of each horizontal bar across, turn.

Row 10: With color B, work lps off hook, **do not turn**.

Row 11: Lng dc post around vertical bar at center of first post sts 4 rows below, pull up lp in top strand of next 3 horizontal bars on last row, *lng dc post around same vertical bar 4 rows below, lng dc post around vertical bar at center of next 2 post sts 4 rows below, pull up lp in top strand of next 3 horizontal bars on last row, rep from * across to last 2 horizontal bars on last row, lng dc post around same vertical bar 4 rows below, pull up lp in last horizontal bar, turn.

Rows 12–28: [Rep rows 8–11 consecutively] 5 times, ending last rep with row 8.

Row 29: Ch 1, sl st in each horizontal bar across. Fasten off. ∎

number 99
continued from page 106

Row 8: With color A, pull through 1 lp on hook, [yo, pull through 2 lps on hook] across, **do not turn**.

Row 9: Ch 1, sk first vertical bar, *sc lp in top strand of each of next 3 horizontal bars, pull up lp in center ch of next ch lp on row before last, sk next horizontal bar on last row, rep from * across to last 4 horizontal bars, sc lp in top strand of each of last 4 horizontal bars, turn.

Rows 10–28: [Rep rows 2–9 consecutively] 3 times, ending last rep with row 4.

Row 29: Ch 1, sk first vertical bar, sc in top strand of each horizontal bar across. Fasten off. ∎

number 100
continued from page 107

Row 29: Ch 1, sc in top strand of first horizontal bar, insert hook in first long horizontal strand on row before last and in next ch sp on last row at same time, yo, pull lp through, yo, pull through 2 lps on hook, sc in last ch of same ch-2, [insert hook in next long horizontal strand on row before last and in next ch sp on last row at same time, yo, pull lp through, yo, pull through 2 lps on hook, sc in last ch of same ch-2] across. Fasten off. ∎

Winter Toque

design by Minette Collins Smith

FINISHED SIZE
Adult's one size fits all.

MATERIALS
- Red Heart Super Saver medium (worsted) weight yarn (5 oz/260 yds/141g per skein):
    1 skein each #4313 aran fleck and #4334 buff fleck
- H/8/5mm double-ended hook used for photographed block
- Tapestry needle

4 MEDIUM

GAUGE
5 sts = 2 inches; 4 rows = 1 inch

PATTERN NOTE
Read General Instructions on pages 5–7 before beginning pattern.

INSTRUCTIONS

HAT
Row 1: With buff, ch 38 pull up lp in 2nd ch from hook, pull up lp in each ch across, turn. *(38 lps on hook)*

Row 2: With aran, work lps off hook, **do not turn**.

Row 3: Ch 1, sk first vertical bar, pull up lp in each vertical bar across, turn.

Row 4: With buff, work lps off hook, **do not turn**.

Row 5: Ch 1, sk first vertical bar, pull up lp in each vertical bar across, turn.

Rows 6–87: [Rep rows 2–5 consecutively] 21 times ending last rep with row 3.

Row 88: Ch 1, sl st in each vertical bar across. Fasten off.

FINISHING
Matching sts, sew first and last rows tog.

For top, weave buff through ends of rows, pull tight to gather. Secure end.

Fold ends of rows up on other side for cuff. ∎

Hooded Blanket

design by Sandra Miller-Maxfield

FINISHED SIZE
45 inches square

MATERIALS
- Red Heart Super Saver medium (worsted) weight yarn (solids: 7 oz/ 364 yds/198g, flecks: 5 oz/260 yds/141g per skein:
    - 4 skeins #4334 buff fleck
    - 3 skeins #336 warm brown
- Size I/9/5.5mm double-ended hook or size needed to obtain gauge
- Tapestry needle

4 MEDIUM

GAUGE
3 sts = 1 inch; 10 pattern rows = 3 inches

PATTERN NOTES
Read General Instructions on pages 5–7 before beginning pattern.

Join with slip stitch as indicated unless otherwise stated.

SPECIAL STITCH
Single crochet loop (sc lp): Insert hook in next ch, yo, pull lp through, yo, pull through 1 lp on hook.

INSTRUCTIONS

BLANKET
Row 1: With warm brown, ch 130, **sc lp** (see Special Stitch) in 3rd ch from hook, sc lp in each ch across, turn. (129 lps on hook)

Row 2: With buff fleck, work lps off hook, **do not turn**.

Row 3: Ch 1 (counts as first st), sk first vertical bar, sc lp in each vertical bar across, turn.

Row 4: With warm brown, work lps off hook, **do not turn**.

Row 5: Ch 1, sk first vertical bar, sc lp in each vertical bar across, turn.

Rows 6–146: [Rep rows 2–5 consecutively] 36 times, ending last rep with row 2.

EDGING
Ch 1, sc in each vertical bar across, **do not turn**, working in ends of rows, evenly spacing sts so piece lies flat, sc across, working in starting ch on opposite side of row 1, sc in each ch across, working in ends of rows, evenly spacing sts so piece lies flat, sc across, **join** (see Pattern Notes) in first sc. Fasten off.

HOOD
Row 1: With warm brown, ch 27, sc lp in 3rd ch from hook, sc lp in each ch across, turn. (26 lps on hook)

Row 2: With buff fleck, yo, pull through 1 lp on hook, [yo, pull through 2 lps on hook] across to last 3 lps, yo, pull through last 3 lps on hook, **do not turn**.

hooded blanket

Row 3: Ch 1, sk first vertical bar, sc lp in each vertical bar across to last 2 vertical bars, sc lp in last 2 vertical bars at same time *(these 2 vertical bars will count as 1 on next row)*, turn. *(24 lps on hook)*

Row 4: With warm brown, yo, pull through 1 lp on hook, [yo, pull through 2 lps on hook] across to last 3 lps, yo, pull through last 3 lps on hook, **do not turn**.

Row 5: Ch 1, sk first vertical bar, sc lp in next 2 vertical bars at same time, sc lp in each vertical bar across, turn. *(22 lps on hook)*

Rows 6–25: [Rep rows 2–5 consecutively] 5 times. *(2 lps on hook at end of row)*

Row 26: Working across slanted edge, with warm brown, ch 2, sc in 2nd ch from hook, evenly sp 25 sc in ends of rows across to last row, 2 sc in last row. Fasten off.

Sew to 1 corner of Blanket matching direction of stripes as shown in photo.

EAR
MAKE 2.
Rnd 1: With warm brown, ch 12, hdc in 3rd ch from hook, hdc in each of next 6 chs, dc in each of next 2 chs, 7 dc in last ch, working on opposite side of ch, dc in each of next 2 chs, hdc in each of last 7 chs, join 2nd ch of beg ch-2. *(26 sts)*

Rnd 2: Ch 1, sc in each of first 4 sts, hdc in each of next 5 sts, dc in each of next 2 sts, 2 dc in each of next 5 sts, dc in each of next 2 sts, hdc in each of next 5 sts, sc in each of last 3 sts, join in beg sc. Fasten off.

Sew Ears to Hood sp 3 inches apart.

BLANKET OUTER EDGING
Working around outer edge of Blanket, through both thicknesses of Blanket and Hood, with WS facing, join warm brown in any corner, ch 3 *(counts as first dc)*, 2 dc in same st, dc in each st around with 3 dc in each corner, join in 3rd ch of beg ch-3. Fasten off. ∎

STITCH GUIDE

STITCH ABBREVIATIONS

beg .... begin/begins/beginning
bpdc .... back post double crochet
bpsc ....back post single crochet
bptr ....back post treble crochet
CC.. contrasting color
ch(s) ....chain(s)
ch- .... refers to chain or space
previously made (i.e., ch-1 space)
ch sp(s) .... chain space(s)
cl(s) .... cluster(s)
cm .... centimeter(s)
dc .... double crochet (singular/plural)
dc dec .... double crochet 2 or more
stitches together, as indicated
dec...................... decrease/decreases/decreasing
dtr .... double treble crochet
ext ....extended
fpdc................................. front post double crochet
fpsc .... front post single crochet
fptr .... front post treble crochet
g ....gram(s)
hdc .... half double crochet
hdc dec .... half double crochet 2 or more
stitches together, as indicated
inc .... increase/increases/increasing
lp(s) ....loop(s)
MC...main color
mm ....millimeter(s)
oz..ounce(s)
pc .... popcorn(s)
rem .... remain/remains/remaining
rep(s) ....repeat(s)
rnd(s) ....round(s)
RS...right side
sc .... single crochet (singular/plural)
sc dec .... single crochet 2 or more
stitches together, as indicated
sk ....skip/skipped/skipping
sl st(s).. slip stitch(es)
sp(s) .... space(s)/spaced
st(s) ....stitch(es)
tog...together
tr.. treble crochet
trtr...triple treble
WS .... wrong side
yd(s) ....yard(s)
yo..yarn over

YARN CONVERSION

OUNCES TO GRAMS	GRAMS TO OUNCES
1...............28.4	25 ....⅞
2...............56.7	40 ....1⅔
3...............85.0	50 ....1¾
4............ 113.4	100............3½

UNITED STATES		UNITED KINGDOM
sl st (slip stitch)	=	sc (single crochet)
sc (single crochet)	=	dc (double crochet)
hdc (half double crochet)	=	htr (half treble crochet)
dc (double crochet)	=	tr (treble crochet)
tr (treble crochet)	=	dtr (double treble crochet)
dtr (double treble crochet)	=	ttr (triple treble crochet)
skip	=	miss

Single crochet decrease (sc dec): (Insert hook, yo, draw lp through) in each of the sts indicated, yo, draw through all lps on hook.

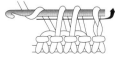

Example of 2-sc dec

Half double crochet decrease (hdc dec): (Yo, insert hook, yo, draw lp through) in each of the sts indicated, yo, draw through all lps on hook.

Example of 2-hdc dec

Reverse Single Crochet (reverse sc): Ch 1. Skip first st. [Working from left to right, insert hook in next st from front to back, draw up lp on hook, yo, and draw through both lps on hook.]

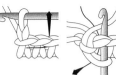

Chain (ch): Yo, pull through lp on hook.

Single crochet (sc): Insert hook in st, yo, pull through st, yo, pull through both lps on hook.

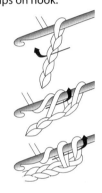

Double crochet (dc): Yo, insert hook in st, yo, pull through st, [yo, pull through 2 lps] twice.

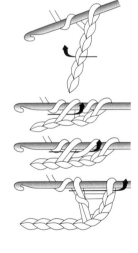

Double crochet decrease (dc dec): Yo, insert hook, yo, draw loop through, draw through 2 lps on hook) in each of the sts indicated, yo, draw through all lps on hook.

Example of 2-dc dec

Front loop (front lp) Back loop (back lp)

Front Loop   Back Loop

Front post stitch (fp): Back post stitch (bp): When working post st, insert hook from right to left around post st on previous row.

Back   Front

Post of Stitch

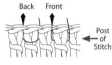

Half double crochet (hdc): Yo, insert hook in st, yo, pull through st, yo, pull through all 3 lps on hook.

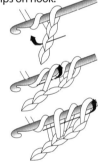

Double treble crochet (dtr): Yo 3 times, insert hook in st, yo, pull through st, [yo, pull through 2 lps] 4 times.

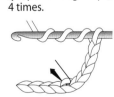

Treble crochet decrease (tr dec): Holding back last lp of each st, tr in each of the sts indicated, yo, pull through all lps on hook.

Example of 2-tr dec

Slip stitch (sl st): Insert hook in st, pull through both lps on hook.

Chain Color Change (ch color change) Yo with new color, draw through last lp on hook.

Double Crochet Color Change (dc color change) Drop first color, yo with new color, draw through last 2 lps of st.

Treble crochet (tr): Yo twice, insert hook in st, yo, pull through st, [yo, pull through 2 lps] 3 times.

Metric
Conversion
Charts

METRIC CONVERSIONS

yards	x	.9144	=	metres (m)
yards	x	91.44	=	centimetres (cm)
inches	x	2.54	=	centimetres (cm)
inches	x	25.40	=	millimetres (mm)
inches	x	.0254	=	metres (m)

centimetres	x	.3937	=	inches
metres	x	1.0936	=	yards

INCHES INTO MILLIMETRES & CENTIMETRES (Rounded off slightly)

inches	mm	cm	inches	cm	inches	cm	inches	cm
1/8	3	0.3	5	12.5	21	53.5	38	96.5
1/4	6	0.6	5 1/2	14	22	56	39	99
3/8	10	1	6	15	23	58.5	40	101.5
1/2	13	1.3	7	18	24	61	41	104
5/8	15	1.5	8	20.5	25	63.5	42	106.5
3/4	20	2	9	23	26	66	43	109
7/8	22	2.2	10	25.5	27	68.5	44	112
1	25	2.5	11	28	28	71	45	114.5
1 1/4	32	3.2	12	30.5	29	73.5	46	117
1 1/2	38	3.8	13	33	30	76	47	119.5
1 3/4	45	4.5	14	35.5	31	79	48	122
2	50	5	15	38	32	81.5	49	124.5
2 1/2	65	6.5	16	40.5	33	84	50	127
3	75	7.5	17	43	34	86.5		
3 1/2	90	9	18	46	35	89		
4	100	10	19	48.5	36	91.5		
4 1/2	115	11.5	20	51	37	94		

KNITTING NEEDLES CONVERSION CHART

Canada/U.S.	0	1	2	3	4	5	6	7	8	9	10	10½	11	13	15
Metric (mm)	2	2¼	2¾	3¼	3½	3¾	4	4½	5	5½	6	6½	8	9	10

CROCHET HOOKS CONVERSION CHART

Canada/U.S.	1/B	2/C	3/D	4/E	5/F	6/G	8/H	9/I	10/J	10½/K	N
Metric (mm)	2.25	2.75	3.25	3.5	3.75	4.25	5	5.5	6	6.5	9.0

Annie's Attic®

101 Double-Ended Hook Stitches is published by DRG, 306 East Parr Road, Berne, IN 46711. Printed In USA. Copyright © 2010 DRG. All rights reserved. This publication may not be reproduced in part or in whole without written permission from the publisher.

RETAIL STORES: If you would like to carry this pattern book or any other DRG publications, visit DRGwholesale.com

Every effort has been made to ensure that the instructions in this publication are complete and accurate. We cannot, however, take responsibility for human error, typographical mistakes or variations in individual work. Please visit AnniesCustomerCare.com to check for pattern updates.

ISBN: 978-1-59635-322-0

1 2 3 4 5 6 7 8 9